nowhere *for* very long

nowhere *for* very long

THE UNEXPECTED ROAD
TO AN UNCONVENTIONAL LIFE

brianna madia

HarperOne
An Imprint of HarperCollins*Publishers*

 For information, address HarperCollins Publishers, 195 Broadway, New York, NY 10007.

HarperCollins books may be purchased for educational, business, or sales promotional use. For information, please email the Special Markets Department at SPsales@harpercollins.com.

FIRST HARPERCOLLINS PAPERBACK EDITION PUBLISHED IN 2023

Library of Congress Cataloging-in-Publication Data is available upon request.

ISBN 978-0-06-304799-0

23 24 25 26 CPI 10 9 8 7 6 5 4 3 2

TO MY MOTHER

for showing me her go-go boots

These stories are pulled from my memory of them, which is as messy and imperfect as the stories themselves. Dates and dirt roads and state lines tend to fade into one another after all those years beneath the desert sun.

All two-legged characters who appear in this book have had their names changed to protect their identity.

nowhere *for* very long

Cattle almost always walk in a line. Even the open-range ones out beyond the fences. Like trained trail horses, they trudge, head down, with the rump of another cow directly in front of them, their narrow trails weaving through sagebrush and patches of prickly pear cactus. A few bulls up in front know exactly which watering hole or feed bucket or patch of junipers they are heading toward and exactly when they expect to arrive. The rest are just in line, head down, hoping for the best.

I made a mental note of this as I watched a herd of them cross the dirt road a few feet in front of my old Ford van. Her thirty-three-inch off-road tires and bright orange paint job *almost* offset the fact that she was about as big and reliable as a junkyard school bus. I leaned forward to rest my chin on the steering wheel, my three dogs barking wildly over my shoulder.

The midday August sun beat down on their dusty black backs; flies swarming, tails swishing. We weren't going anywhere anytime soon. Not because of the cattle, of course, but because the van in which we sat had been broken down right there on that road for over twenty-four hours.

The day before, I had loaded up enough food, water, and supplies for two weeks out in a remote southeastern corner of the Utah desert. I left early, driving west from the town of Moab toward Capitol Reef along a two-lane, sun-bleached highway. After an hour or so, I hooked a hard left onto a dirt road before slowing to a halt in a plume of dust. I got out, locked the hubs, checked the ratchet straps on the roof rack, got back in, and shifted into four-wheel drive.

Forty-eight miles later and forty-eight miles from pavement, the van rolled silently to a stop in a network of desolate dirt roads. There had been no loud clanking noise, no odor of leaking fumes, no smoke from the hood. A tie rod end hadn't snapped, jerking the wheel ninety degrees and sending me skidding violently into a sandbank. Rusted leaf springs hadn't cracked in half, rendering the van slightly crooked and limp as though the passenger side had had a stroke. (All things that had already happened up to that point, by the way.) I cranked the starter a few times, pumping the gas pedal with each attempt, but there was no sound besides the cicadas buzzing in the heat.

I jumped out of the front seat—still a far fall even at my five-foot-ten stature—and squatted down to look at her undercarriage. Above my head was the orange and black nameplate I'd had custom-made for her front grille. *Bertha*. Named after my favorite Grateful Dead song.

Her front axle seemed intact. There were no hanging wires or dripping fluids. Nothing felt overheated beyond the usual searing hot steam that billows up from the belly of a thirty-year-old van. I lay on the ground and used my feet to slide myself across the sand beneath her like a mechanic without a dolly. With my eyes, I scanned all the parts I knew. The brake drums and the rotors and the shocks and the drive train and the exhaust system.

Sand from the ground stuck to the sweat on my skin even when I stood to lift the front hood. Again, I scanned. The radiator and the alternator and the transmission and the oxygen sensor. I could name all of these parts, but I couldn't repair a single one of them. That had been my husband's job, back when I had a husband. And for a girl who'd traded in just about everything for that old van, you'd think I would have at least bothered to learn how to fix it.

The nearest mechanic shop was 190 miles away. That's what the woman on the other end of the phone said when I called for a tow service. I had climbed on top of Bertha to get a better signal. The operator's voice cracked in and out as I paced on the roof rack next to the solar panel. She said she would contact me when she found a flatbed tow truck that was willing to make the near-four-hundred-mile round trip. She had no guarantee of when they would come or if they would come at all.

When I hung up, I felt strangely calm. I suppose when there had been two of us standing roadside with this broken van, there were sharp words and blame to throw around. He would say that I should have known the van wouldn't make it this far. I would say it would have been fine if he had fixed the right part. He would say it was my decision to live in this fucking thing anyway. And it was. It was my decision. And now it was just me left to reckon with it.

Perhaps that sense of calm came from the realization that there was no longer anyone there to say *I told you so.* No longer anyone there to try to convince me to give up on Bertha, because for some ungodly, inexplicable reason, I just could *not* give up on Bertha.

I climbed down, slid the door open, and watched the dogs burst out across the field in search of the jackrabbits that come out at dusk. They disappeared from view as I yanked the cork from a wine bottle with my teeth and took a good, long swig.

For as many times as I had watched the sun dip low in the desert, it still mesmerized me. First the pale blue turns to pink, softening the edges of all the sharp, brambly desert things. Then the reddish-orange seems to rise up from below like fire, silhouetting the hills and the junipers and the sandstone cliffs. Then just like that, it dims and fades and the dogs wander back to the van and the deep blue night drips down over us.

Even as I stood there in the middle of the road beside that giant orange mess of metal, it all seemed so peaceful. There had been no dramatic explosion, no horrible screeching car accident, no burst of fire consuming her whole. Bertha just rolled silently to a stop one day on a completely nondescript dirt road that sliced through a sagebrush field, and it was over.

That part of my life was over.

I believe the truth of how we become who we are is layered. Not like onions, but like earth. Traceable at the surface, but tumultuous beneath. Tectonic plates of our pasts shifting violently, or more often subtly, causing great rumbling disruptions in the identities we think we've mapped so well.

I didn't grow up in the desert. I didn't grow up in any kind of world where risk was encouraged, where fear was celebrated. In fact, living in an old van with only the coyotes for neighbors was a positively rebellious departure from my middle-class Connecticut upbringing. A middle finger to the only way of life I'd ever witnessed. Grow up. Go to school. Get a job. Get married. Buy a house. Have some kids. Make a lot of money. Buy a bunch of stuff. Work constantly to afford all the stuff. And then hope you're still alive and able-bodied enough to go out and see the world.

Where I came from, how much you had was always more important than who you were. Wealth was not measured in the stories you could tell, but in the price of your car and the size of your house. And it wasn't ever the concept of *wanting* all that stuff that turned my stomach. I understood wanting; it was the sickness of *wanting* all that stuff so badly and so often that I might forget to go find what I *needed*. It was the insatiability of it all; that no amount of anything was ever going to be enough because I hadn't found what enough truly felt like. So, I set out to prove what I didn't need. My quest for simplicity started with a summer spent living on an old, mildew-covered thirty-foot sailboat before I fled west to Utah with the boyfriend who eventually became my husband. Then we made a home out in the desert in that big orange van, where the echo of our voices on the canyon walls were the closest sounds to civilization.

We were a ragtag group of misfits. Modern-day traveling gypsies. The big orange van named Bertha with a propensity for back roads and breakdowns. The steely-eyed hound named Bucket with ears soft like mullein weed. The unruly little dingo named Dagwood, adopted and returned three times before he made his way to us. My husband, Neil, whom I'd known since I was just ten years old. And me, of course, just desperately trying to document it all, because forgetting it was my greatest fear. The five of us became so intertwined, we practically wore each other on our skin. Dog hair and desert dust and Bertha's black engine blood dried deep in the cracks of our knuckles. But even the most beautiful stories can have tragic endings. They can also have beautiful endings. Though I suspect any story worth telling has a little bit of both.

I never would have imagined that I would end up alone, but perhaps it was inevitable. Perhaps it was just one more thing I had to prove. In many ways, Bertha was the most important thing in my life, and I chose her over the things that probably should have mattered more. But there was something about that van that felt like a critical extension of myself. It was a getaway car from whatever I was running from. It was a representation of the risks I had taken. It was some sign of success that I had done it. I had escaped the mundane confines of the "American Dream," even when my own version of it was sitting crippled and immobilized in the middle of nowhere.

From the top of the van on that hot August night, I scanned the horizon, marveling at the nothingness in every direction. Maybe that should have scared me, being alone and stuck out there. But in that moment, I scarcely cared if a tow truck arrived at all.

I took another swig of wine as the juniper trees began casting their long evening shadows. I could hear the dogs yipping at the heels of a jackrabbit. In the distance was another long line of cattle, weaving like a freight train through the dust. I sat and watched as they disappeared over a hill, one after another after another after another.

It had been a very long time since I had walked with my head down.

PART I

We must be willing to let go of the life we have planned so as to have the life that is waiting for us.

—JOSEPH CAMPBELL

The tide always determined how difficult it would be for my dog, Bucket, to claw her way up the metal ramp at the base of the dock. At low tide, it was practically vertical and my boyfriend, Neil, and I would push her by her haunches while she awkwardly clambered at the rungs. At high tide, it was flat as dirt and she'd prance right over. No matter the tide, fishermen busied about, throwing us a wave as we made our way up toward the parking lot each morning. Neil and I would walk hand in hand, discussing our schedules for the day or what we might have for dinner that night. We were on our way to work like any other couple, but there was no rush. Time just never felt real until our bare feet left that dock. Piping plovers with their toothpick legs scurried through the mud alongside us, pecking at snails and cracked mussels, flapping their delicate wings territorially as we passed. Fiddler crabs side-scuttled in frantic herds beneath the wooden planks at the sound of our approach. Bucket would pause to watch them sometimes, tilting her velvet hound ears from side to side. For all its quirks and oddities, living on an old sailboat on this dock was the only home that dog had ever known.

There was nothing in my early years that might have suggested I'd end up living that way. I was born and raised in Fairfield County, Connecticut, just about an hour outside of New York City. It's a place known for its over-the-top wealth and, subsequently, for its over-the-top wealth disparity. Within Fairfield County are the town of Fairfield and the city of Bridgeport. And despite their being geographically flush up against one another, the average household income in Fairfield was about triple the average in Bridgeport.

The little blue house I grew up in sat perfectly—and precariously—on the line of those two places, in a small neighborhood called Black Rock. I could drive down my street, take a left, and run into a million-dollar waterfront home, or I could drive down my street, take a *right*, and run into government-subsidized housing projects, or the charred frame of a burnt-down home that nobody bothered to rebuild.

Black Rock was still *technically* Bridgeport, but for the most part, it was a pleasant little middle-class place with flower beds in front yards and families on bicycles and a paved pathway that wound around the water of Long Island Sound. Old folks played chess outside the neighborhood market, and kids carved their initials in the oak tree in front of the big house on top of the hill before someone came out and shooed them away.

Every bike I'd ever had as a kid was stolen. One day when I was twelve, I borrowed my brother's without asking. I rode down to the corner store for candy, but when I came out not five minutes later, it was gone, and I was hysterical. A man I recognized from the neighborhood told me to jump in his truck. He had seen a kid taking off on a red bike.

Miraculously, we found him pedaling frantically down a side street. I watched nervously through the windshield as the man nearly ran him off the road before jumping out and throwing him to the ground. The boy on my brother's bike couldn't have been much older than me. A white kid with a dirty, oversized T-shirt and a wallet chained to his belt loop.

Break-ins and shattered car windows and pillaged center consoles were just as common. I have vivid memories of friends not wanting to ride the public bus with me because they were far too frightened of the kind of people who needed to. One year, a schoolmate's mother refused to let her come trick-or-treating with me. "All the kids from Bridgeport come over there," she grimaced.

Hordes of teenagers would arrive on presumably stolen bicycles with pillowcases to fill with candy; not the freshly purchased plastic pumpkins the other kids carried around. Even on a day meant for dressing as something you're not, some folks still couldn't escape the identities they had been assigned.

My mother would wave to the neighbors and the kids on the stolen bikes from her eternal position amid the flowers in our front yard. No zip code could keep her from pruning the petunias to perfection, but even she carried a sense of shame that we couldn't afford to make it over the geographical and metaphorical line. She was adamant about writing *Fairfield* on informal address forms. "Close enough," she would whisper to me under her breath.

My brother and I went to private schools in different towns, because the public schools in Bridgeport had metal detectors at each entrance and a noteworthy teen pregnancy rate. So, each morning, we would battle our way up into the front of my dad's work van. Whoever didn't shout "Shotgun!" fast enough sat on the center console with their legs dangling. We'd stop by Dunkin' Donuts first and then tumble out the door in front of the redbrick school building behind the church with pink frosting smeared across our cheeks.

I knew we were different in some way, but I was too young to know exactly why. I had a few guesses. I could feel my cheeks flush when other parents would stare. Perhaps it was the lack of seat belts or the sawdust sprinkled across our uniforms or the faint smell of marijuana embedded in the fabric of Dad's seat cushions. He was a contractor and my mother was a school secretary. I can't imagine they made a whole lot of money, but they worked tirelessly to give my brother and me the life they believed we needed. Money was the only thing I really remember them fighting about. Dad made too little of it and Mom spent too much of it, which was easy to do, I suppose, when trying so diligently to keep up with the neighbors. The waterfront-home neighbors, of course, not the subsidized-housing neighbors.

And so that's how I grew up—right in the middle, more of a chameleon than a pack animal. Not quite rich, but not quite poor. Not from the right neighborhood, but not really from the wrong one either. Close enough to press my hands to the glass and peer inside, but far enough to know exactly which side of the glass I was on. Even as a child, I learned that it mattered. For some reason, it mattered deeply where and how you lived.

My mom never viewed me so much as a child she'd given birth to, but as a friend she'd been waiting her whole life to meet. When I was growing up, she and I would dance barefoot on the hot pavement in rainstorms or hop the fence to someone else's pool and jump naked off the diving board beneath a ghost-white moon. It was as though that cloak of silvery darkness provided enough safety for her to disregard where we were in the neighborhood pecking order, if only for a moment. When she and I were together, there was nothing else in the world.

One school night, she burst into my bedroom and threw open my dresser drawers looking for something for me to wear. Her friend was supposed to go with her to an Aerosmith concert but she was sick, so my mom slicked some lipstick across my twelve-year-old face instead.

She drove us over to the amphitheater, where we sat in the front row. So close, in fact, that I reached my tiny hand up onto the stage where Steven Tyler paused to let me touch his strange satin slipper. I'd never been to a concert before. My mom cheered and sang and danced in too-tight leather, grabbing my hands and swinging me from side to side beneath flashing lights.

When my mom was in high school, she would leave the house in the morning in the dresses her mother laid out for her, but as soon as she was safely on the bus, she'd unzip her backpack and pull out faded jeans and the white patent-leather go-go boots she kept hidden under her bed. She embodied the in-between. It seemed as though she wove effortlessly between two spaces at once. She was a complicated woman, as most of us are. In many of my childhood memories, I recall her caring deeply about what other people thought. In many others, she seemed to disregard it entirely.

One summer afternoon when I was in middle school, she and I rowed a small boat out into a creek surrounded by mansions with sprawling wraparound porches. Without warning, she stood from the bench seat, steadied herself, stripped off her clothes, and jumped stark naked into the water in broad daylight. "Who cares?!" she shouted, floating on her back, laughing, motioning for me to join her.

I suppose I should have been embarrassed by a mother who jumped naked into neighborhood swimming holes, but I loved her most in those moments, when the Connecticut housewife costume slipped off and she just was who she was.

Sometimes I think I resented the world I was raised in so much because it was stealing a part of her from me. I'd search her face at church gatherings or Christmas cookie exchange parties or in the aisles of the supermarket where she'd stop to chat with *Mrs. So-and-So*. She looked so different to me there: stiff and rehearsed, as if playing a role. Beneath it all, I saw a woman free and naked, moving effortlessly through water pierced by midday sunlight.

The woman I truly looked up to—idolized even—was the one with the go-go boots hidden in her backpack.

When I was ten, my family was approved to join a local yacht club that we most likely couldn't afford. Kids took swimming and tennis lessons while stay-at-home moms and full-time nannies lounged by the pool, peering up occasionally from magazines to watch the lean, oiled bodies of lifeguards reprimanding their children for running on the deck.

It was there amid that positively clichéd Connecticut world that I first saw Neil. He was twelve years old, hanging off the side of a little white sailboat. Painfully shy, he spent much of our adolescence avoiding eye contact beneath a bed of curls, tinted brassy blond from the salt of Long Island Sound. In our high school years, we sailed together on a team called "Big Boats." An old, white-haired member of the yacht club named Mr. Lander would arrive in his bright red Porsche and escort a group of sun-tanned, dull-eyed teenagers onto his multimillion-dollar sailboat to teach them how to race in regattas.

We were ordered to wear white polo shirts and khaki shorts, and if we were efficient and civilized, or better yet, if we placed in the regatta, we were rewarded by getting to watch Mr. Lander have a celebratory beer and shift his hips side to side to the crooning of Jimmy Buffet's "Margaritaville" as we sailed back into the harbor.

I was fourteen and would have rather been just about anywhere else on earth. Mr. Lander complained often about the shortness of both my khakis and my attitude. My unwillingness to learn affirmed my position on the sailboat. I and a few other kids were assigned to sit on the deck with our legs hanging over the edge to balance out the weight of the boat when we were heeling to one side in strong wind. I was, in short, extra weight. About as important as a bag of sand.

Neil, however, was a sailing prodigy. At the age of fifteen, he was often at the helm of the ship, gazing upward at the telltales atop the towering white mast, shifting the smooth wooden wheel ever so slightly beneath his hands as the sails billowed with new pockets of wind.

He was known for taking a tiny one-man sailboat out in gale-force knots, steering the bow directly into oncoming storms, crashing through whitecaps, and heeling so far over the side that only his feet remained on the boat. One evening, with the wet white spinnaker sheet wrapped tightly around his fist and a hurricane on the horizon, he heeled so hard against the raging winds, he broke his own back.

A raised and jagged purplish scar from mid-spine to tailbone serves as a permanent reminder of a kid who lived like he had nothing to lose. But I'd have never guessed that the skin beneath his old Bob Dylan T-shirts bore markers of such ferocity.

He was soft-spoken with a honeyed voice. Filled with liquid courage on Friday nights, he'd pluck expertly at his guitar onstage with his high school band, then disappear out a back door before anyone even knew he was gone. That was how I knew him. Calm, like the surface of the water we'd shared out on bows of great white boats. Mysterious, like long scars hidden below cotton tie-dye.

One summer evening, I was home from my sophomore year of college when I stopped by a friend's house for a barbecue. Neil was seated across the table from me, fidgeting with the label of his beer bottle. I had always thought he was handsome.

"Do you ever see Mr. Lander?" I asked.

He glanced up at me and smiled. Despite our shared childhood, we had hardly ever spoken more than a few words to each other. But there in the backyard that night, weighed down with summer heat, something had shifted. We talked for hours.

His parents had moved out of state, leaving him nothing but their old thirty-three-foot sailboat, *Satisfaction*, floating in the murky brown waters off Long Island Sound. And in the summer of his twenty-first year, that's where he lived. It was fitting to know he still existed there in the only place I'd ever really known him; sun bouncing off mirrored waves, salted hair, terra-cotta skin. It was as though he had stayed there, frozen inside the memories of my childhood. The boy on the sailboat.

When the party was over, we stood beneath the humming of a streetlight. Timidly, he asked if I'd like to come down and see the boat. He seemed almost shocked that I agreed. We spent that first night together down there on the dock, hands awkwardly fumbling over one another as though we were still the wide-eyed kids we'd known each other to be. The following day, mere hours after we'd parted, a text message lit up the blue screen of my flip phone. It was Neil.

Want to go sailing tomorrow? For old times' sake?

Some beginnings happen so fast, they hardly feel like beginnings at all. One day Neil asked me to go sailing; five weeks later he told me he loved me as I stood barefoot in the street, tear-soaked and waving as his car disappeared out of sight. He was bound for Plattsburgh, New York, where he would spend the next three years getting a degree in expeditionary studies while I returned to the University of Rhode Island six hours away.

He would call me in between classes. Mine: technical writing, poetry, and English literature. His: emergency survival, white-water kayaking, and ice climbing. We were as different as we'd always been, but we'd slipped seamlessly into each other's worlds as though we had lain dormant there all along.

We would drive hours through the night, seeing who could orchestrate the best surprise. Who could pop out from behind someone's dorm room door or appear on the other's quad after class on a Friday like in some cheesy eighties movie.

Despite the fact that we talked on the phone constantly, he would write me letters; long, handwritten letters on pages ripped from his notebooks. He'd draw pictures in the margins and list all the things he loved about me.

After I graduated two years later, I made my way up to Plattsburgh with a five-pound box of letters resting on the front seat beside me. The corners were dog-eared and worn from all the times I'd left a college party to lie in my bed and reread them.

We spent his final year of college in the upstairs apartment of a multifamily home that should have been condemned three families ago. Making eight bucks an hour at a bagel shop and living in a beer-encrusted, black-mold-infested apartment with six college guys wasn't exactly what I had in mind for postgraduate life, but I'd have roped the moon for Neil. One evening, as his graduation date approached in the spring of 2012, I stared at the dull glow of my computer screen. I had $301 in my bank account and $40,000 in student loans. We were embarrassingly unprepared for a reality we had known was coming.

As of May 1, we had nowhere to go. We had no safety net to fall back on, no childhood bedrooms to move back into. Neil's parents had moved to Pennsylvania years ago, and my mother was renting a small bedroom from a Hungarian woman with a little dog named 22 (pronounced *Two Two*). What remained for us were the floating bones of that old sailboat, *Satisfaction* . . . the one we'd fallen in love on that summer off the coast of Connecticut. Neil's parents planned to sell it, but they begrudgingly agreed to let us live on it while we worked to save up some money. In exchange for their kindness, he would do some maintenance on the old family heirloom.

In theory, it was simple, and on paper it looked downright glamorous. But reality set in quickly as we teetered down the wooden dock our very first night, dragging bags of our belongings, dancing around chunks of decaying crabs dropped and cracked open by the gulls. Cockroaches flitted across our feet, disappearing from one wormhole into another. The stench of low tide was unmistakable.

A sliding hatch door in the stern of the sailboat revealed a small wooden stepladder down into the cabin. The cushioning smelled of mildew, and the low, swaying lights gave the constant, stomach-churning effect of being far out at sea, despite being firmly tethered to the dock. There was no running water, no internet, no television. The pump toilet had been too expensive for us to get working again, so a trip to the bathroom meant climbing up the ladder, off the boat, down the dock, through the gate, into the marina parking lot, and over to a small bathhouse near the karaoke bar.

We fell into a hushed silence as we unpacked our backpacks that first night, squeezing past each other in the twenty-eight-inch-wide hallway, bickering over space in the single wooden drawer that would contain our clothing. As I bent down to pull out my toiletry bag, a cockroach the size of my palm came up with it. It must have caught a ride on my backpack when I'd set it down on the soggy wooden planks.

Once eye-level with it, I shrieked and tossed the small zippered pouch into the air, sending it flying across the cabin. Seconds later, the cockroach took flight, and not simply because the object upon which it rode was careening through the air. He spread the wings we had no idea he had and launched forward toward my face.

Screaming and wildly flapping our arms, we ran circles around the crawl space we were to call a house for the next seven months. From outside the boat, I imagine our shrieking sounded like something out of a horror movie, but nobody came calling to see what the fuss was about. All the other boat owners were tucked far away in their mansions while two kids on a dimly lit dock attempted to make a home in a slip between their weekend toys.

We stayed awake for hours afterward, laughing and drinking until our eyelids were heavy, sharing our first sleep—of countless more—with our heads pressed together on a tiny triangle-shaped cushion beneath the bow in the unavoidable company of cockroaches.

As summer wore on, life on the dock began to seem quite normal. Above the cushion we called a bed was a small, clear hatch window through which we welcomed the world each day. I needed only to open my eyes and look straight upward to know what awaited us.

Some mornings, we woke to vivid blue sky and puffy cartoon clouds, the sounds of squabbling seabirds and the hollow clanging of sheets against the mast. Some days we woke to the stench of thick mud and mollusks floating through the cracked hatch, a telltale sign that the tide was out and the dock would be dotted with the remains of blueback herring or, if the gulls had been lucky, a meaty horseshoe crab.

Some days—my favorite days—we woke to the sound of raindrops on the hull, the sky a deep stone-gray. Tucked beneath permanently dampened blankets, we'd reach up and trace fallen streaks of water down the glass and drift back to sleep as harbor waves lapped at the fiberglass.

Save those rainy mornings, the only running water we had came from a faded green hose shared between our boat and the neighboring slip. Air-conditioning wasn't an option, which left the thick East Coast humidity hanging dense in every corner of the boat. Rarely was there a time when we didn't have a thin veil of sweat across our skin. A small icebox served as our source of refrigeration, but the only things it ever really held were beer and leftover rice and broccoli from my favorite Chinese place. We had one burner, one pot, one pan, two cups, and various pieces of plastic silverware from said Chinese restaurant that we would wash and reuse. For entertainment, we would make up songs, or play Scrabble, or jump naked off the dock into the dirty harbor water.

It was as though we'd stepped into a different world, a different time. There, amid the grandeur and the wealth and the opulence of the place where we had both grown up, we existed inside our own little bubble. It was an intentional way to live. There was nothing to drown out the sounds and the smells and the discomforts around us. I could not shut a door when it was too loud. I could not push a button on the wall when it was too cold. When it rained, I heard every drop like pennies on a tin can. When the heat rolled in, it wrapped itself heavy around every limb. When the great fat gulls belted out their brittle morning calls, I heard each note. When the sun rose, I rose with it, unable to block out the light from the mirrored reflection of glassy harbor water.

It brought about a kind of presence in the mundane routine of my day-to-day life that I hadn't known before. Never before did I have to figure out the most basic of human comforts, because they had always been a completely mindless part of my existence. But this? This was a totally different kind of being alive. This was complicated, but in the same breath, it was so exquisitely simple.

I have, for as long as I can remember, been deeply drawn to animals. My childhood was spent in a dilapidated old pet store down the street from my school. The owner let me clean the cages and hold the animals and give him bags of quarters to save the feeder mice from mouths of snakes.

In fact, over the years, I brought home half that damn store. Two dogs, three cats, six birds, two snakes, a tree frog, a tadpole, a chameleon, and about fifty various rodents. The only thing my mother didn't let me keep was a hairless rat that I tried to sneak home in my backpack without her noticing. She said it looked like a scrotum.

I'd wander around my neighborhood with parakeets on my head and mice in my pockets and a snake around my wrist like a bracelet. Recess at school was spent catching ladybugs, and weekends were spent down at the end of my street feeding the geese. They'd grown so used to me that they'd stomp their leathery feet right up onto my legs as I sat there in the grass with scraps of crackers and bread crusts.

Our neighbors eventually had a meeting about my behavior, as the geese had begun to wander up the block, leaving their droppings on everyone's lawns. I was just happy to know they had come looking for me.

Photos of my childhood were filled with horses and frogs and dragonflies and salamanders and birds. Always birds. Baby chickadees that had fallen from nests and broken-winged sparrows pried from the jaws of our cats.

When I was ten, I found an abandoned swan egg left in a matted pile of reeds. My parents knew from the smell that it was never going to hatch, but they let me bring it home anyway. I wrapped it gingerly in a nest of old beach towels beneath a heating lamp borrowed from the chameleon. And then I waited desperately for my baby to hatch. When it didn't, I was devastated.

I always dreamed of being a mother bird.

I was twenty-one years old when I lied on an application at an animal shelter, claiming my boyfriend and I lived in a big, beautiful house in the nice part of town when we really lived on that thirty-three-foot sailboat with no bathroom, no air-conditioning, and no running water. I knew they'd never send that little brindle hound home with two kids floating on a boat in Long Island Sound. In their eyes, I had absolutely no business adopting a dog.

So I lied, and they bought it, and that's how I became the mother to my first little wild thing.

We named her Bucket, which raised almost as many eyebrows as our living situation. Neil and I had decided on the name one evening over beers at a local brewery a few months earlier. With a good buzz going, we grabbed a napkin and a pen from my purse and decided to write a bucket list of things we were going to accomplish by the end of our lives. The following morning, Neil pulled the crumpled napkin from the pocket of the jeans he'd fallen asleep in. On it, it simply read: *Get a dog, name it Bucket.*

She was about six months old and almost entirely legs the day we brought her home. The cracks between the wooden planks terrified her, so Neil carried her up and down the dock for the first few days until I spent one afternoon on my own hands and knees, crawling in circles, demonstrating to her how safe the wood was. She stared at me blankly from a blue seat cushion on the bow. Other boat owners stared at me from their own slips with equal confusion.

It took only a week for her to accept this strange new reality, and another week to become downright jovial about it. She would lay her long, brown-brindled body on the warm wood hatch cover in the stern of the boat or dangle her front paws over the edge of the dock, watching intently for the flap of a fish tail. She chased the seagulls with such enthusiasm and purpose, you'd never know she hadn't ever actually caught one. Ironically, she was—and still is—nervous in what most dogs consider very natural situations. Walking past strangers on leash, navigating fenced-in dog parks, cars passing too close to ours on the highway. But sleeping on a sometimes-violently rocking sailboat, leaping five feet down from a dock to a dinghy, swimming in deep, dark water far from any shoreline . . . she was completely at ease. She looked to me for everything, trusted my every move. All I had to do was nod, and she knew she was safe.

I got a job working weekdays as a nanny for a local family who'd been kind enough to let me bring Bucket along. The lack of air-conditioning inside the sailboat meant it was impossible to leave her alone for the day without turning her into a rotisserie chicken.

Our daily routine was simple. She and I would wake each morning and sleepily wander down the dock toward my red Jeep Wrangler. Earlier in the summer, Neil and I had lifted the hard top off and left it in a quiet corner of the boatyard. But when the weather called for storms a week or so later, we returned to find it had been stolen. So my Jeep sat topless for the rest of the summer, cup holders filled with rainwater, seats bleached with sun.

Still wearing my pajamas, I'd drive a few blocks over to my storage unit, giving a wave to the employees loitering near the loading dock. They knew Bucket by name and no longer gave a second thought to the barefoot girl in a bathrobe punching in her key code. Once inside, I'd grab a rolling metal stepladder and push it down the hall, rusted wheels squeaking and dragging with each turn. My unit was about the size of a closet, but slightly deeper. It was stacked on top of another unit, hence the stepladder. I'd unfurl the thin garage-like door, coax Bucket up the steps and into the box, and then slide the door down behind us both.

I kept a small battery-powered lantern on top of one of the plastic Tupperware bins. I'd fumble for the switch and use the dim glow to choose my clothes, strip down, and get dressed. I had learned the hard way that stuffing my belongings into a singular wooden drawer on a humid sailboat resulted in a lasting mildew smell even the toughest detergent couldn't remove. So, climbing up inside a makeshift metal closet seemed a better alternative, albeit a much stranger one.

I often wonder what Bucket was thinking, spending four or five mornings a week inside a big, dark box for several minutes. She would sit there, staring blankly ahead, as if it were the most normal thing in the world.

Once dressed, I'd drive over to a café to buy my breakfast of black coffee and a banana while Bucket barked at passersby in the parking lot. One morning, a barista who had come to know me well suggested that I could probably save myself some money if I just bought a bunch of bananas at the supermarket instead of buying one there every day.

"Oh, I would love to," I laughed, counting out coins, "but I live on a boat and my boyfriend says we can't have any bananas on board because it's, like, an old pirate curse or something . . ."

Owning a sailboat sounds fancy enough, but living on one? Visions of glistening white million-dollar catamarans with white-suited deckhands probably danced through her head. Perhaps we had family money, inheritances. Perhaps we'd stumbled into great wealth at our tender young ages. Whatever her suspicions, one thing became clear to me that summer: I was uncomfortable with the assumption that we were rich. In fact, I often went out of my way to correct anyone who might think so. I flaunted my chipped fingernails, my worn out T-shirts, my lack of even the most basic amenities. It was an odd departure from the mindset I'd grown up with. In Fairfield County, appearances were everything. And if you couldn't *be* rich, you should at least *look* rich. When I turned seventeen, my mom surprised me with a humble four-door sedan she had gotten from a used-car lot. I recoiled at the sight of it. My classmates drove tricked-out SUVs and BMWs. "I wouldn't be caught dead in a car like that," I scoffed.

It sat, untouched, in front of our apartment for three days before my mother got the folks at the dealership to take it back. She returned with that used red Jeep Wrangler instead and hurled the keys across the room at me before slamming her bedroom door.

I used to feel sick thinking about that. How obnoxious, how spoiled, how utterly skewed my idea of what was important was at such a young age. How many seventeen-year-olds would have killed for that perfectly good sedan?

I try to look at that girl today with a kinder perspective. I was born and raised in the in-between—at the center of shame and guilt and money and status. Of course I wanted to trade in and trade up. Everything in my young life was up for improvement and negotiation; I had no loyalties to anything but upgrades. It was all I knew.

But, to this day, I still own the red Jeep. Nearly half a lifetime later, I can't bring myself to get rid of it. I don't want to seem ungrateful. It felt like the smallest penance I could pay to hold on to it all these years. Guilt is funny like that.

Neil spent that summer teaching sailing lessons to kids a few towns over at another yacht club. The folks he mingled with each day were a bit more accustomed to boats and banana curses. He would return to our dock each evening, darker than when he'd left. The deep leathery brown of his skin was stark against the white boat deck. He would sit on the starboard side with his legs dangling above the water and play the guitar while I cooked dinner on the propane stove.

Sitting beneath the sail, we'd scoop rice and veggies into our mouths straight from the pot, waiting for the swans to swing by and beg for our leftovers. Over time, they learned to take them directly from our outstretched hands. And over time, Bucket learned that she had to share these treats with the great white-winged dogs or they'd snap at her without hesitation. Once finished, we would sit out on the edge of the dock and wash our dishes with a hose and a bottle of biodegradable soap.

The setting sun offered us a chance to discreetly wash our naked bodies down with that same hose, battling the evening mosquitoes. Anything to save a trip to the parking lot bathroom.

Climbing down into the cabin, we'd leave the hatch open with the prayer of a breeze. When it was too hot to sleep, we'd lie side by side up on the bow, shaking with laughter at the drunken karaoke renditions of "Sweet Caroline" and "Don't Stop Believin'" that echoed out over the water from the dive bar.

On weekends, we would throw off the bowlines, open the rainbow-striped jib sheet, and sail out into the open water. Out past the moorings and buoys. Out past the sunbathers and lobster traps. Out past the little white lighthouse and the jet-black cormorants sunning themselves on the rocks below. Out past the yacht club where we'd grown up. On calm, windless days, we could hear the sounds of the children we once were leaping off the old, faded blue diving board. We'd head out toward Long Island, keeping the three smokestacks on the right side of the dunes to our north.

Bucket would stand on the bow in her polka-dotted life jacket, hound ears flapping in the wind. We rigged a little pulley system to lower her down into the water so she could join us for a swim in the heat of the afternoon sun. It was always a funny sight when she swam out in the open sea. She wasn't quite sure what the objective was, so she would just make splashy little circles around us with her tail as a rudder.

It was the very picture of contentedness. The kind of memories that flood your eyes with sun flares and fill your chest with salt air. Sometimes we'd go out for hours. Other times, we'd go for days. Always sailing back in after watching the sun melt over the horizon, turning all the towns we knew into blackened silhouettes against the sky.

It began to feel as though we had a secret down there at the end of that dock. As though we had discovered a loophole we weren't supposed to find. The more time we spent floating out there, the more I felt myself slipping from that silhouetted world we had grown up in. I felt, very suddenly, like a visitor in the places I'd called home. An imposter in the conversations I'd once conducted.

I had spent the summer watching a rat-race world from the bobbing of a boat, subconsciously documenting the kind of life I *didn't* want. I didn't want the job in the city and the cars and the kids and the yacht clubs and the tennis lessons and the picket fences. These were dreams someone else dreamed for me before I even knew who I was.

"What on earth do you have against picket fences?" my mother once asked. In retrospect, it wasn't too terrible of a question. But it was never the picket fences themselves that bothered me; it was the competitive display they represented. Beyond the pearly white posts and the prizewinning rose gardens were overworked fathers and dead-behind-the-eyes, daytime-Chardonnay mommies, and little brats like myself demanding nicer cars, fancier clothes, more extravagant birthday parties. Nobody wanted to talk about the shadowy parts of this life that seemed so blindingly obvious to me.

I was away at college when I read the news about a man from back home. The IRS was coming for his fortune. The opulent life his wife and children had grown accustomed to was about to be gone. So, one evening he came home from work, loaded his handgun, and shot his entire family one by one before turning the gun on himself.

In fact, when the stock market crashed in 2008, men all over the tri-state area started blowing their heads off, swallowing bottles of pills, flinging themselves from eleventh-story windows onto the pristine pavement of Wall Street. Better dead than poor.

Now, who's to say there weren't extensive underlying circumstances in each of these cases, but as an impressionable eighteen-year-old, it was staggering. There were so many people who believed life was no longer worth living without wealth . . . that plummeting to your death in a three-thousand-dollar suit was better than applying for food stamps or driving a used car. As a young adult, I stashed this away in my subconscious until I found myself reaching exclusively for the things money couldn't buy. Boat, Neil, Bucket—these were the best things in my life, and each of them was a nail in the coffin of traditional wealth. I'd lived through what I was supposed to believe was the scariest thing—life without money, security, comfort—and found it wasn't so scary after all.

Something about that boat felt more real, more human. We had spent just seven months of our lives existing in the way millions of people do for the entirety of theirs. No excess. No convenience. No luxury. And yet, alongside this invigorating new desire for a life of less, I also became acutely aware of the inherent privilege in *choosing* to struggle. In *choosing* to move backward in a world full of forward. You see, we're all born somewhere along the assembly line with the same shining goalposts at the end. Wealth and success and beauty and opulence and *stuff*. Lots of stuff. Being born in middle-class

Connecticut, I just so happened to have the advantage of being closer down the line toward those goalposts than most. Surrounded by people who were "born on third base and thinking they hit a home run," as Mary Karr's late father used to say.

And it was there, when I was reasonably within reach of all that, that I came to realize I wanted none of it. After all, the closer you are to the masterpiece, the more you see the cracks in the paint.

By the end of October, the nights had begun to grow colder, and rumors swirled of a potentially devastating hurricane heading up the East Coast. One evening, as we sat eating dinner, a young kid who worked at the marina came jogging down the dock toward us. Bucket was startled by his pace and began barking nervously. The sky had already begun to glow an ominous purplish gray.

"The police just posted evacuation notices all over the place," he huffed, out of breath. "I think you guys should get out of here, the marina owners are gonna lock the gate."

Within hours, we'd silently packed what little we had into a couple of backpacks and tossed them on the dock beside the boat. We loosely and lovingly tied as many of her lines to the dock as we could, placing all of the big rubber bumpers on the side we could envision being thrashed against the dock.

Over the next few days, we hunkered down at Neil's brother's house as ninety-mile-per-hour winds whipped by like freight trains outside the windows. The streets began to fill with water as Hurricane Sandy pounded the Connecticut coastline. Trees uprooted as easily as blades of grass, ripping up entire lawns with them. Businesses flooded. Million-dollar waterfront homes were swept away.

A friend from high school posted a photo of a black-and-white linoleum kitchen floor floating in the Long Island Sound. I could see the outline of where the appliances had been. People had worked their whole lives to build a world that made them feel successful, made them feel safe. Within a matter of minutes, it had been tossed to the sea.

Even when the winds died down and the rains ceased, the sky swirled in a thick gray haze for days. We ventured out through a completely powerless town, looking out the car window at shattered glass storefronts, splintered branches, flooded intersections, and swinging power lines.

We wound our way through the destruction in an attempt to get back to the dock. Once there, we sprinted to the waterline, weaving through a row of mutilated boats, toppled over like fiberglass dominoes. Through the gated entrance to our slip, I could see that half of the dock was gone. Some boats were floating aimlessly in the water out beyond, while others lay smashed up against the rocky harbor shore. By some bizarre miracle, there, in the surreal calm of post-storm waters, *Satisfaction* bobbed right where we had left her.

The relief was overwhelming, but with the immediate threat of devastation out of the way, reality set in. The storm had spared us, but the season was over. Boats that hadn't already been taken out of the water would need to be in the coming weeks. Ice would start to creep in from the muddy marina corners, and the thick beads of heat that hung in the air belowdecks would soon turn to frigid New England frost. We were, once again, without a home and without a plan. Back to square one, as though we'd dreamt it all up. And yet, the fragility of those seven months on the boat had always been part of the appeal. We knew we couldn't live that way forever, and that's what we loved about it. There was a newfound thrill in the impermanence of our choices.

We drove back to Neil's brother's house and opened our individual bank accounts on separate computer tabs. We had saved just under five thousand dollars between the two of us. We figured that was enough to get us somewhere new. The next morning, with the power still out and the storm drains still draining, we headed over to my storage unit on the other side of town. Two employees out of uniform were assessing the damage of a downed tree in the parking lot when we arrived. One of them immediately recognized Bucket. I explained that we were trying to leave town, but with the power out, I wouldn't be able to get inside using the keypad.

"Wait here," one said.

A few minutes later, we heard a loud banging at one of the loading garage doors as the two of them pried it open and guided us in.

"I guess we could have brought you through the employee entrance," one smiled, "but we've got to keep some kind of protocol around here, right?"

Flashlights in hand, we followed Bucket down the darkened hallway. The building had flooded only slightly, but I was suddenly grateful for the squeaky metal stepladder I had fought with all summer. Once in front of my unit, the guys told us to call them if we needed any help.

As Bucket splashed about in the inch or so of water on the floor, Neil and I proceeded to load two black garbage bags full of clothes and one small plastic bin of mementos I had held on to. Posters from my college dorm room. Photo albums from high school. Neil's letters. The following morning, I tearfully hugged my mother on the street in front of the house she rented a room in. "You can always come back," she cried, as I inhaled the scent of her. But I think she knew I wouldn't.

It was a strange way to leave the place I'd known all my life. National Guard and police vehicles regulating a now postapocalyptic-looking town, strangers fistfighting in hours-long lines at gas stations. Bucket watched through the window, perched like a queen on a throne of black garbage bags in the back seat. We weren't sure we'd even make it past Pennsylvania. Eventually, a Shell station appeared in the distance with only three or four cars in line. We turned in, shut the engine off, and waited. In the tension of that moment, I was comforted by the thought that most everything I had was within arm's reach.

We filled up as much gas as we could before slipping out of sight amid the chaos and confusion, moving on like the last winds of a passing storm. We had settled on Salt Lake City, Utah, for reasons I still can't quite recall. All we knew was that rent was cheap and mountains were close. I grew up looking out into the flatness of a watery horizon my whole life. Mountains felt like the epitome of adventure.

I wish I could tell you we weren't scared. I wish I could tell you the fear didn't grow exponentially with each passing state line. But it did. The farther we went, the more real it became. Sometimes I wonder what my story would have been if I had saved up diligently for an apartment after college . . . if my childhood bedroom had been waiting for me . . . if I had made some sort of five-year plan and stuck to it. Sometimes I wonder if living on a musty little sailboat would ever have been my choice if I felt I had another. I was so unsure of myself those first few weeks down there at the dock. As unsure as I was right there on that flattened freeway on the way out west. But it became comforting to think of fear as a vessel of freedom. I had scared myself right into the kind of life I wanted.

We spent two days inching through thick traffic outside of New York City, then New Jersey, then Pennsylvania, where the cities started to melt away and the grass stretched out over rolling hills, abbreviated only by deep wooded stretches and picturesque red barns. The haze from gridlocks of car exhaust and factories gave way to blue sky and gilded grass and storms I could see coming from miles away.

We made our way through Ohio and Indiana and Illinois and Iowa, seeming to gain ten extra feet of sky with every passing mile. When we crossed into Nebraska, I was asleep. Neil rubbed my arm as the sun was rising, drenching everything in melted pink. A flock of tiny pointed-wing swallows came diving through the sky in front of our car and floated along with us for a good while, as if we were just one of the birds, drifting along silently on feathers we didn't know we had.

I woke up differently that day. It was as though the two-hour upright nap I'd taken at four in the morning with my face pressed against the car window had been the most transformative rest of my life. Like I'd spent twenty-one years battling for space and elbowing my way through crowds and struggling to hear the sound of my own thoughts and weaving through pavement squares of steaming vehicles filled with faces all staring up at buildings and bridges and skyscrapers . . . and now? Nothing.

We had punched through the membrane of the giant, turbulent cell of the part of the world we called ours for so long. We had drifted clear out of our own atmosphere, floating in slow-motion, looking back at everything spinning-spinning-spinning on without us. Out here no one knew our names. No one cared why we were stopped. We were just two kids on the side of the highway in Nebraska, leaned up against the front of the car watching the sun light up a stretch of sky we'd never seen before.

We crossed into Wyoming in a snowstorm so thick, the state threatened to close Interstate 80. It was November, and we listened to Obama's reelection announcement over the radio before the crackle of the emergency alert system broadcast its warning. We splurged on a thirty-five-dollar motel room off the freeway, gawking at posters for a *Youth Sheep Wrangling Contest* in the lobby. The nonsmoking room reeked of cigarettes and the television wouldn't turn on, but it was still an upgrade from sleeping in the back of the car with our legs in the trunk and our backs propped up awkwardly on the folded-down seats.

After a hot shower, I pulled the covers down to find one single macaroni noodle tucked into the bedsheets, its neon-orange cheese stain seeping from all sides. We stood over it solemnly as though we'd just discovered someone's remains. Then we looked at each other and laughed.

I suppose it's odd that I felt so proud lying in a sleeping bag on the floor of a motel room with someone else's dinner tucked into the bed I paid for . . . but I was proud. This was the farthest I had ever been from home, the most daring adventure I had ever taken. For as long as I'd been alive, I'd listened to people talk through their teeth about all the trips they would take and the hobbies they would pick up and the books they would write and the bands they would start, only to watch those dreams get stacked away in old boxes behind record collections and dusty picture frames. I lay there on the floor that night smiling from ear to ear. I was not going to be one of those people.

The following morning, the storm was still blinding. Nevertheless, we rolled along with a slew of big-rig truckers going an average of thirty miles per hour in whiteout conditions. We had meant to stop and take a photo in front of the big WELCOME TO UTAH sign, but the fact that we could even see it through the snow as we passed six hours later was a miracle in and of itself.

Moving to Utah was by no means glamorous at the time. In fact, everyone we knew outright laughed at us when we mentioned that we were even considering it. The only thing folks in New England knew about Utah was that those wacky Mormons had claimed it as their own personal promised land. That, and the skiing wasn't terrible. The only thing *we* knew about Utah was that we could actually afford to live there.

Neil shrugged off all the same tired jokes about low-percentage beer and multiple wives, but I grimaced at the teasing. Utah didn't exactly feel like the great escape I'd always dreamt of. I had assumed I would end up in California.

Growing up in New England, California just *sounded* like freedom. Long-haired surfers and pot-smoking San Franciscans and bikini-clad girls on boardwalks. But one scroll through the classified ads proved that there wasn't a single dog-friendly apartment we could afford. The vision I'd long had of tearing off down the highway toward the iconic haze of the California coast faded rapidly from my mind, and that felt like some sort of failure.

I realized then that it was going to take some time to shake the stranglehold of comparison culture from my bones. Utah wasn't California, but it wasn't Connecticut either. And I had no intention of being the girl who never left home.

I found us a pet-friendly four-hundred-square-foot studio apartment on Craigslist for $485 a month. It seemed too good to be true, and it very well could have been, considering the fact that we had blindly sent the deposit to a person I had only spoken to via email. We drove all the way across the country simply hoping it actually existed. It was still snowing hard when we finally arrived, carrying our bags precariously up the stairs.

Bucket ran back and forth inspecting every inch of carpet, but I walked directly to the kitchen sink and turned on the faucet. I swiped my fingers through the warm, flowing water. It was a luxury I had never considered a luxury before I'd lived without it. The gratitude for something so simple felt like an accomplishment in and of itself.

For the next three days straight, it didn't stop snowing for a single moment. We dragged a mattress up the stairs in the snow. We carried out bags of kitchenware from Target in the snow. We stared out the window at the snow. It was as though we had moved into a snow globe that someone just wouldn't stop shaking. Which way was up, down, east, or west was anyone's guess.

On the third morning, I awoke from the mattress on the floor to an eerie sliver of blue sky behind the bedroom curtain. We tripped over each other, grabbing mismatched gloves and socks and still-dampened jackets from the floor. Bucket leapt eagerly from the mattress to the couch, waiting for the door to open. The sun bouncing off of several feet of snow was so blinding, it took a few moments for my eyes to adjust. We looked up the nearest dog park and set off down the road.

About eight hundred feet from our apartment, we rolled to a stop at a red light. And there, off to the left, over some glowing McDonald's arches and an orange Home Depot sign, were the Wasatch Mountains. It was strange, I suppose, to be sitting at an intersection amid strip malls and fast-food joints with tears in my eyes. The streets were quiet. We sat through a whole second cycle of the stoplight. Green, then yellow, then red. Just staring, staring up at those mountains. It was as though someone took any old city in the country and hung a huge painted canvas of granite, snow-covered peaks directly behind it. It hardly looked real. They stretched on in great, rolling droves to the north and the south and floated up thirteen thousand feet to the bluebird sky. The jagged summits were so close to the clouds, it seemed they might pop them if they passed by too low.

Over the next few weeks, we ran around feeling toy-sized beneath the enormity of all that sky, slowly burning through all the money we'd saved in cheap Chinese takeout and tanks of gas that took us up into the mountains that framed the valley we now called home. We'd marvel at their massiveness; the way they seemed to stretch on, eternal. Bucket would track through the trees and meadow grass, new smells and sounds and sights reverberating off of her every movement. I would watch her, awestruck, wondering what lay beneath the surface of the domesticated dog I'd known . . . what lay beyond the far-off horizon I had to squint south to see.

Eventually, with nothing but a few cans of soup left in the cupboards and a few hundred bucks left to our names, we began searching for jobs. Side by side in coffee shops, we'd peer over a shared laptop screen as snow fell outside the windows, crystalline and blinding.

I scored an interview for an account management position at a telemarketing research company. I teetered awkwardly into the lobby in high heels and a blazer I'd purchased the day before from a bustling downtown mall. Clutching the black folder containing my embarrassingly sparse résumé, I waited. I had gone to college, I had been a nanny, and I had worked at a bagel shop. I was honest about those shortcomings with the soft-spoken Mormon man who interviewed me. He told me that one of the managers there had come from a background of stocking shelves at Walmart.

"I know you're from the Northeast," he said, smiling, "but out here, some folks still believe in working your way up from the mailroom."

Three weeks later, when I was down to my last few dollars, he called to offer me the job. My starting salary was $28,000 a year, and for a twenty-two-year-old with zero experience, I thought I had just about struck gold.

Neil landed a job with a wilderness therapy company—the

kind of work he'd long dreamed of doing. A rising trend in the mental health field, these companies aimed to provide thirteen- to seventeen-year-olds with an alternative treatment environment, fostering self-efficacy and healthy autonomy. At least, that's what it said on their websites.

The reality of the industry had far more dirt under the fingernails. General field staff, like Neil, would spend eight-day shifts sleeping, eating, and living alongside groups of adolescents who would almost certainly rather be *anywhere* else than the desolate wilderness they were confined to, either by their parents or by a printed order from a juvenile court.

Dull-eyed, angry kids were given string and piles of sticks and instructed to make their own backpack upon which they would carry their assigned belongings. When they wanted to cook, they had to start a fire with their own two hands, whittling sticks together until their fingers were blistered and raw, until the shavings of the sapling began to smoke and jump with each frantic rotation. When they wanted to eat what they'd cooked, they had to carve their own spoon from the branches of the juniper trees that stretched on, endless, in every direction.

Neil would arrive home at the end of each eight-day stretch, exhausted and filthy, but buzzing with a sense of purpose. We'd curl up on our faded blue thrift-store couch and collapse into the shape of each other, sharing the details of the different worlds that would keep us apart for more than half of each year.

During those eight days when Neil was out working, there were no phone calls, no text messages, no emails. Just silence. I'd wake up alone and come home alone and cook alone and fall asleep alone. Of course, I had Bucket, who became my reason for doing just about everything. I'd force myself to go out to the dog park with her to try to meet people, to try to feel some sense of belonging. But it was lonely. I'd write down lists of things to tell Neil when he got home, little mundane things I didn't realize made up a whole life when someone was gone. Things like *Show Neil funny dog video* or *Play Neil new Lord Huron song* or *Tell Neil about awful conference call.*

Sometimes it felt like I was living everything twice; once when I experienced it, and again when I was retelling it to Neil. I imagine my propensity for storytelling grew further in those years. In the years when even the most uneventful things became things worth remembering.

I was standing in a Petco across the street from our apartment with my arms wrapped around a bag of Bucket's kibble when I first saw him. He was a golden fawn of a thing, fifty some-odd pounds with big, sturdy paws and dark-rimmed eyes. He looked, for lack of a better description, exactly like a wild dingo.

The clipboard hanging from his crate said his name was Dagwood. I stared down at him, but not once did he look up at me. There were no fireworks, no eyes-locking, heart-stopping moment. He didn't even notice that I was there. His paws dug frantically at the bottom corner of the metal crate. He would pause and pace inside the tiny walls, panting in anguish, before resuming his digging in that same corner, now scarred with white claw marks like chalk on a blackboard.

Quite suddenly, his desperation to get out became my desperation to get him out. My heart pounded against the bag of dog food I peered over. It felt as though it was me in that crate. Panicked and frantic and stuck. But I left him there. The rental agreement on our apartment said we could only own one dog. So I left him there.

The following morning, unable to get the golden tips of his ears from my mind, I called the number on the shelter card I had swiped from the table before leaving the store. The volunteer who answered the phone informed me solemnly that a family had come in and adopted him later that afternoon. Probably just an hour or so after I had left.

I was strangely crushed to have lost him, though he'd never been something I'd had. Deep in my gut, I knew it was a death of what should have been. For weeks I couldn't shake it. My coworkers would catch me staring at his photo from the shelter on my computer. I'd taken a screenshot of it before they removed it from their website. On long hikes after work with Bucket, I would squint my eyes and imagine what their two tails might have looked like bobbing along next to each other, what his eyes might have looked like all lit up out there in the wild.

A little over a month after I'd walked out of that Petco, Neil arrived home from his shift with a surprise. He had called and spoken to the apartment manager, and they had given us approval to get a second dog.

"I thought we could go up to that same shelter from the adoption event," he said softly, ". . . see if they have any other dogs like him."

The following weekend, we drove half an hour north of the city down an industrial road past warehouses and salvage yards until a small animal shelter appeared among them. Wide-eyed cats watched from the windows as we followed the walkway to the front door.

At the reception desk, an older woman with a long gray ponytail greeted us and offered to show us the dogs they had available. As she stood from her chair and reached for a jumble of key chains, I asked quietly, "Did Dagwood go to a good home?" She paused and sat back down. Peering over the top of her glasses, she flipped through some loose papers on the desk, then held one up to her nose.

"He did," she said, before dropping the paper back to the desk, "but it looks like they brought him back. Poor guy. That's the third time someone's brought him back."

She stood again, reaching for the keys, before noticing that Neil and I were frozen in place. Looking from his face to mine, mine to his, she asked, "Do you want to see him?"

Dagwood burst through the door in a plume of golden fur, long, slender snout to the tiled floor. He was thin and fox-like, but he dragged that volunteer across the room with sheer stifled energy vibrating off his haunches. Again, he hardly noticed us.

When his leash was unhooked, he sprinted from side to side, nearly ricocheting off the walls, pausing only to rotate his satellite ears toward what might be another dog passing in the hallway.

We brought Bucket in from the car to introduce them, but Bucket never fancied herself much of a dog. She was regal, but nervous, and spent most of that initial visit glancing from wall to wall, wondering if it was she who was going to be left behind this time. Dagwood came barreling in to her face, sniffing frantically before losing interest immediately and diving into a bin of dog toys on the other side of the room. Bucket sat motionless, perplexed.

Dagwood moved so erratically across the room that it was hard to get a good dead-on look at his face. Neil reached out and cupped his snout between his hands and held his gaze for a few seconds. His eyes were deep and almond. One had black eyelashes; the other, white. Below his nose was a tiny black Charlie Chaplin mustache.

The volunteer reemerged with a clipboard in hand and sat down across from us as though she was about to deliver a critical diagnosis. "Dagwood has had quite a history," she said. "He has been adopted three different times by three different families in his first year. He is . . . a handful. He's very playful with other dogs and loves people, but he is destructive and has proved to have major issues being potty trained. He shouldn't be around small children, as he's just far too excitable, and he will most certainly maim or kill any cat or small household pet due to an exquisitely sharp prey drive."

She scanned down the page with her finger and finished, "The last family who brought him back were keeping him in their bathroom because they didn't know what else to do." She stood abruptly to walk back out of the room before turning at the door, adding, "Oh, and our maintenance guy wanted me to tell you that Dagwood jumped up and chewed through the pulley that opens the door to the outside portion of his kennel so they couldn't put him back inside. He doesn't like being inside." And with that, she walked out.

Neil and I turned to each other with the same amused smile. Dagwood had calmed down considerably and now stood staring at us in anticipation as if to say, "So, when do we leave?"

We adopted Dagwood for the discounted price of seventy-five dollars that day, most certainly under the assumption that we'd be back to dump him off in a few weeks like everybody else. But Dagwood never saw that place again. He flitted around our studio apartment shoving his snout into the garbage and pulling open cabinets with his little lion paws. Bucket watched stoically from the couch as he ransacked our belongings.

In an effort to quell some of his insatiable energy, we loaded both dogs into the car and headed for a large off-leash network of dog trails at the base of the Wasatch Mountains. Bucket padded along beside us cautiously, as she always did, steering clear of strangers. Dagwood, who was still on a leash at the time, lunged in every direction until we thought he might snap his own neck. Every dog that passed by needed to be greeted, and then mounted, and then humped before we desperately pried him off. The two were quite the odd couple. Calm and chaos. A mouse and a wolf.

Once in the center of the park and without any moving distractions in sight, we unclipped Dagwood from his leash and held our breath. He turned to look at us just once before sprinting full-speed into the forest and out of sight. We stood with our jaws agape, staring blankly at the space between the naked winter trees where he'd disappeared.

Neil screamed his name at the top of his lungs before I gently reminded him that he probably didn't even know what his name *was*. We ran toward the tree line, embarrassed and panicked, sweating through the underlayers of our winter jackets, calling out the name of a dog who didn't know his name.

Suddenly, about a hundred yards up the trail, a woman called out, "Is this your dog?" Bounding along beside her pack of Bernese mountain dogs was Dagwood, slack-jawed, tongue flapping, eyes bright. He caught sight of us and sprinted our way in a moment of recognition.

Neil snatched him by the collar and pulled his nose in toward his own. "You have to stay with us," he said, firmly. And for the rest of the walk, Dagwood did.

That's how it went for the first few months. Dagwood bouncing off the walls until we freed him from them. Every afternoon when I got off work, I'd take the dogs somewhere, anywhere, to run. Nose to the ground, he moved through every landscape with Bucket in tow as though he belonged, as though he'd always been there. In certain light, he startled people, terrified them even. On remote mountain trails and sloping cliffside tallis fields, women yelled out and men jumped back. Children pointed innocently at his shadowed outline moving against the horizon, shouting, "A coyote!" or "Look, Mama, a fox!"

Sometimes I kept silent, wanting them to believe it for a moment longer. Wanting to believe it myself. Wanting to possess, in some small way, the wildness he represented.

But that wildness came with a price, as most wildness does. The moment our apartment door closed behind us with Dagwood left inside, he tore up anything he could find. He chewed at the wooden blinds until the couch was sprinkled with sawdust. He broke every baby lock on every garbage can and littered the carpet with coffee grounds and food scraps. He dragged bags of potatoes around the house and buried ripe avocados in the couch cushions. He shredded magazines and packages and cookbooks. He tore down the Christmas tree, shattering nearly all the ornaments. He pooped on the floor not out of an inability to hold it, but out of pure unadulterated spite. This was proven one day when I forgot my lunch for work and drove back to the apartment a mere ten minutes after I had left. Dagwood sat staring at me beside a fresh steaming pile of petulance.

One evening at the dog park as I sat exhausted, watching Dagwood mounting every other male dog in the place in an ultimate quest for dominance, a woman approached me and pointed at him.

"Looks like an American dingo." She smiled. Having heard the old "dingo ate my baby" line more times than I cared to count, I smiled and mumbled flippantly, "Yeah, we hear that a lot."

She sat on the bench next to me and put her hand on my arm, "No, it's a breed! It's a real thing! You should look it up, your boy looks like the poster child for it." Back in my car with the dogs curled on the seats, I pulled out my phone and typed "American dingo" into the search bar. What I held in my hand were pages and pages and pages of Dagwoods. I clicked the first link and read aloud to myself:

The American Dingo, or Carolina Dog, is a primitive breed of dog only domesticated as recently as the 1970s. It is generally theorized that these dogs are descendants of ancient breeds from Asia that traveled with nomadic tribes across continents over the Bering Strait.

A man named Dr. I. Lehr Brisbin studied these dogs extensively, especially their mitochondrial DNA. "If they were just dogs," he said, "their DNA patterns would be well distributed throughout the canine family tree. But they're not. They're all at the base of that tree where you find the most primitive of dogs. After centuries of selective breeding, to see a Carolina Dog is to glimpse a dog molded and sculpted only by natural selection. It is *Dog* in its most natural form."

I suppose that was when it hit me. There was a reason I felt something practically primal when I saw Dagwood for the first time, when I finally got to see him running wild, and that is because he quite literally *was*. And yet, despite the newfound knowledge that we had some sort of primitive dog living in our studio apartment, we still attempted to adjust him to a city life. The caliber of trainers we needed, we couldn't afford, and the trainers we could afford just couldn't change him. We found a doggy day care facility that accepted both him and Bucket, even though Bucket would have rather just lain on the couch at home. Still, when I'd pick them up, Dagwood's little "report cards" would read that he'd gotten into a fight or he'd been removed from the play yard for humping, or he'd flipped the baby pool over for the fourth time this week.

The only things that ever calmed him down were being outside and being with us. He understood the rules of a pack. It was trust, not tyranny, that got his attention. He'd look up at us with shameful eyes beside a huge pile of mail he had shredded, knowing he'd done something wrong, knowing we were disappointed, but he never stopped. I suppose we could have tried to break him; to send him away or even send him back, but I had a strange sense he was trying to tell us something about the way we were living. *There's more to it than this,* he said.

He didn't need a walk in the park. He didn't need doggy day care. He didn't need an occasional hike or swim in a lake. He needed something much more. Sometimes I think he knew that I did too.

When I was sixteen, my brother left for college at Montana State University in Bozeman. Now, Bozeman, Montana, might as well have been called Bumblefuck, Nowhere. It would have been exactly the same to me. That was one of the jokes I made to my friends over lunch in the school cafeteria. It got big laughs. For a teenager who had scarcely left the bounds of Connecticut, Montana was another planet. One that I didn't have any particular interest in visiting.

Nevertheless, toward the end of his freshman year, my mom and I flew out to visit. We landed at the log-cabin-looking airport and waited for our baggage beneath the watchful gaze of a couple dozen taxidermy elk. I texted pictures to my friends back east constantly.

The sky was so wide, it was practically disorienting, but when we got into downtown Bozeman, I was surprised by how charming it was. Boutiques and ice cream parlors and folks sitting out on patios drinking local beer. The houses on the outskirts were all brightly colored with porches full of college students, their faces buried in books.

One night—when he needed a break from towing his mom and little sister around—my brother went out to a party with some friends. Back in our motel room, my mom sorted her meticulously packed suitcase looking for a bathing suit. She had made small talk with a local at the grocery store who told her about a remote little hot spring an hour away. Reportedly, there was live music and a little shack that served booze.

We drove up and out of the bounds of the street signs and stoplights of Bozeman into the rolling Montana plains, the setting sun sinking faster with each mile. Falcons floated overhead in the last light of dusk, their expansive wings barely moving on the breeze. Deer shot out across our headlights what felt like every other minute. Mom gripped the wheel tighter. I could hardly believe a road like this even needed to exist. It had been at least forty minutes since we had seen another car or stoplight or street sign. They may as well have left it a field full of deer.

We arrived at the hot springs just after sunset, stripping our clothes off in the gravel parking lot next to the car. The sound of a guitar was unmistakable. The tub was shaped like a large sunken living room, with benches all the way around and open space to float in the middle. Tattooed, dreadlocked folks sat with beers in their hands, bopping their heads along with the musician on the platform of pallets they were calling a stage. The entire tub was made of wood that had worn down and smoothed over time. It was so soft, I could have mistaken it for sand. Steam rose up around us like a cocoon.

We sat side by side, our heads laid back on the cold pavement, looking up at the stars. "There's so many of them," I whispered.

"Just think of all the ones we can't even see . . ." she whispered back.

On the drive back toward town, I stayed staring up at the stars, the wet hair on my forehead pressed to the window. The tips had become little blond icicles before we'd even reached the car. The only things that pulled my eyes from the constellations were the occasional lights that would appear out in the distance, glowing from the windows of tiny houses. If I squinted, I could make out the flickering glow of a television screen, a truck in a driveway, the darkened silhouette of a horse behind handmade fences of wood and wire.

"Who the hell would want to live all the way out here?" I laughed. "Probably some serial killer. Like, imagine driving hours to the fucking grocery store?"

My mom smiled and shrugged, her eyes glued to the single tunnel of pavement glowing in our headlights.

After my parents divorced, my mom was always coming up with these little excursions for us to go on. Mostly around the holidays. I think she tried to distract me from the fact that it was usually just her and me now. We'd load up the car, bound for hotels in towns we'd never been to, or bed-and-breakfasts in the middle of nowhere in Vermont that had a reputation for a mean Thanksgiving buffet if you could find your way there. One year we spent Christmas at an old haunted mansion in New Hampshire, trudging through the wooded property to find old red barns where horse-drawn sleighs waited to pull us through the snow.

In those strange and different places, we could pretend to be anybody. We would talk in fake accents or come up with different names for ourselves, different identities. We were heiresses or secret agents or supermodels or food critics or travel journalists. We'd jump on beds and watch true-crime shows and order room service and take the elevator to each and every floor. We *always* had to stay in a place with a hot tub.

In the wake of the divorce, my mother began to seem less occupied with the image she had cared so deeply about. Amid disaster and heartache, she embraced freedom and mischief and laughter and open roads. And she took me with her.

When I looked at her there behind the steering wheel on all those odd and accidental roads, her eyes shone with excitement, but flickers of grief still flashed as frequently as the wild things that darted out into our headlights.

Those aimless adventures changed the way I looked at things, right down to a stretch of Montana sky and an expanse of horizon I might have previously considered boring. If there was nothing right there in front of me, that didn't necessarily mean there was nothing up ahead. That didn't mean there was not every reason in the world to keep driving.

She changed the way I looked at being different. While there was always a dull, yet deep-seated longing for a "normal" family, those excursions were the first time I felt proud to not have one. Holidays and spring breaks would come and go, and I'd return to school with all kinds of stories to tell my classmates. It sounded lovely, but no one particularly cared that Amanda's grandmother made the same peach cobbler for the twenty-seventh year in a row or that Sara's uncle got drunk again. They wanted to hear about what my mom and I had gotten into . . . how long it had taken us to find that snow-covered barn, or those elusive brussels sprouts hiding in the hills of the north country.

Having spent the majority of my life within the pristine lines of the New England suburbs, that lone highway cutting through the Montana foothills was the closest I'd ever been to any sort of unmarked dirt roads. Any sort of winding interstate going nowhere. I had never driven into nothingness.

All my life, it seemed to me that everything belonged to someone. Every fence line, every gated community, every *No Trespassing* and *Private Property* post furthered my belief that there was nothing really left to discover. There were plots and squares and boundaries and lines drawn and our only option, as civilized humans, was to exist inside of them; to carefully tiptoe around the corners of each other's worlds, casting out any semblance of wildness beyond the bounds of a property line or a freshly mowed lawn.

. . .

It was Valentine's Day the first time I saw the desert. Neil thought it would be good to show me the canyons that kept him from me for nine days at a time. I thought it would be good to let the dogs really stretch their legs. With our sleeping bags laid out in the back of Neil's white work truck, and the dogs fogging up the windows with their eager panting, we headed south.

We rolled along the interstate, tracing the base of the Wasatch Mountains before cutting up into a canyon that would take us to the other side of the range. Snow piled higher and higher on either side of the road as the four-cylinder pickup surged and struggled against uphill stretches. The skeletons of naked trees framed the single-lane road while evergreens loomed farther up each side.

There were no strip malls or billboards, just the occasional RV trailer or closed-up gas station or little wooden house tucked between junkyards of dilapidated cars. It seemed that within just a few miles, we'd left the bustling of a busy valley and ascended up into a place that felt forgotten, or perhaps had never been found at all. I was surprisingly calmed by the thought of what we'd left behind, by the unknown I peered out into beside Neil's assured hands at the wheel.

Once at the summit, snowfields stretched on in every direction, interrupted only by the dark dotting of black cows. "Open range," Neil explained.

As the pavement wound us down, walls of blocky granite began to shoot up beside us, the road bursting through them like the dynamite that put it there in the first place. We rolled down, down, down without a need to press the gas, the sloping of the earth carrying us along just fine. The snow gave way to golden dirt hills and crumbled slopes of rock until the canyon finally spit us out into flat fields framed only by distant buttes; mountain like, but with plateaued tops in bursts of sandstone red.

We passed through quiet little one-light towns with trailer parks and three-aisled grocery stores, always centered around the bright white steeple of a Mormon church. In one of those towns, Neil cut left just past the post office. Pavement turned to gravel and then gravel turned to dirt. The dogs perked up immediately.

For the first five miles or so, it didn't appear that we were going much of anywhere. The fields stretched on in every direction, spotted with spindly juniper trees that reached eight feet high at best. The dead junipers stood like ghosts among the living, with new fledglings growing up around and over and through them, but the haunted limbs remained. In the desert, as with all things I suppose, the only thing more visible than life was death.

Each unnamed dirt road we passed looked the same as the one before it and the one that would inevitably come after. The idea that anyone knew their way around out here was unfathomable. There were no street signs or mile markers. Even the cows looked confused. Then again, cows always look slightly confused.

At a four-way intersection totally void of stop signs, Neil took a right and slowed the truck to a stop. Turning to me, he said, "Look at the time on the clock." It was a little after 2:00 p.m.

"Exactly ten minutes from now, the whole world will be different." He tucked his long hair behind his ear and pulled back out onto the dirt, grinning from ear to ear.

The flatness of the high desert began to give way as we wound down a rutted road. Navajo sandstone rose up on either side until I had to press my face to the window just to look up and see the sky. Boulders the size of SUVs had fallen, shattering and rolling down hillsides. I could see the scars on the walls where they'd once been. Determined little sagebrush poked through the most unlikely piles of debris. Big-horned sheep stared down stoically as we passed. A small wash with the occasional murky brown puddle wove alongside the road—the shadow of what remained of the ancient floods that had shaped this canyon.

As promised, Neil stopped the truck exactly ten minutes later. The dogs leapt from the passenger door and darted off across the dirt. Normally I might have called after them, but I was frozen there in the doorway. In every direction, mazes of sandstone walls each more different and magnificent than the next. Lizards perched unmoving on red rocks, turning their faces toward the sky with eyes shut in utter content, seeking eternal the fleeting February sun.

I squinted out at remnants of grand towers that once stood, now whittled down to a single sandstone pillar, surrounded by slopes of crumbling rocks and prickly pear poking through the dust. In the sand beneath my feet, it was easy to see that it had rained recently, or that perhaps some snow had melted down smooth and slow enough to drag pebbles along, leaving snail-like trails behind them. Like looking down on river tributaries from the window of a plane.

Everywhere I turned there were cracks and crevices and narrow canyons; twisted paintbrush pathways carved deep into the earth by rushing water and passing time. Petroglyphs and pictographs pecked into the pristine rock like canvas. Childlike etchings in muddied red paint of big-horned sheep and coiled snakes. Tall, spindly human figures with outstretched arms and soft S-shaped lines sprouting from each. Capes. Or wings, perhaps.

Neil pointed out a little cave up on a hillside. It was here that he and some students in his program had stumbled upon the remnants of pottery, rough and sanded over, but visibly different from the rocks around them. Unsure of their origin, Neil called in to the Bureau of Land Management, who sent officials out to survey.

What they discovered was that those pieces—some whole, some shattered—belonged to the Diné people and were somewhere between two and three thousand years old. Left there, undisturbed, untouched. Left there, half-buried in desert dust as an entire planet moved on around them. Neil was right. In just ten minutes, the whole world was different. As horribly cliché as it sounds, it felt for the first time that my soul had perhaps lived once before. And if it had, it most certainly lived here.

To step inside this place was to step inside a story already being told. I was not the beginning of anything. I was a speck of dust blowing through. A happening among other happenings. And where that realization may have found others unsettled, I found myself comforted.

As we sat there on that day in February, watching the sun light the tips of the towers pink with the last reach of its rays, I felt a flood of anger. Anger for having gone this much of my life without so much as a hint that this world was here. The desert was a picture that had been painted for me in cartoon pages and old movie scenes. Vast piles of sand, blinding heat, lifeless stretches of horizon. Nothing to see, nothing to do.

But this was different. To be inside those canyon walls was to be cradled in the arms of the earth itself. I felt hidden out there. Safe. As if I could just slip away and be carried off to rest among Indian paintbrush and coyote willow. Left there undisturbed, untouched. Buried somewhere in the sand like pottery.

It is fair to say that we all fell in love with the desert, but none so much as Dagwood. Bucket would hunt for lizards and splash about in muddy streams, and lounge her dark, brindled body in the sand, but Dagwood would disappear into the landscape. Sometimes for hours.

We'd catch sight of him every now and again, slipping between the junipers, calloused paws crunching over cactus and snakeweed. He moved like he belonged here. It was as though he was a puzzle piece that we'd slipped perfectly—finally—into its place.

We began spending every weekend as far deep into the desert as Neil's truck could get us. And when we had driven every road we could find, we drove farther. On a map at my desk at work, I used the bottom of a bottle to draw a circle around our apartment, encompassing everything within a six-hour driving radius. Six hours was what we had deemed reasonable to accomplish on a Friday night after work.

We drove to every desert within that circle, stopping at all the mountains and valleys on the way too, camping on the edges of buttes and climbing up towers and slithering through canyons and marveling in the glory of our dogs just being dogs.

The sound of the dirt roads beneath the tires drove them mad, so we started opening the doors and letting them run out ahead in front of us. *Redneck running* your dog, they call it. They ran faster than the lumbering of our four-wheel drive anyway.

Sometimes they would sprint out in front; sometimes they would tear off to the sides and weave between the brush. Other times, they would run right alongside the van like wild horses. It was their favorite thing in the world.

Sometimes days would go by before we saw another human being. Utah had so much "in-between," as I liked to call it, that it was always possible to be alone. Bouncing minivans of children and Cruise America RVs would motor endlessly between the five national parks, the tourist towns, the hub cities. Like toy cars on a track.

And tucked down unmarked dirt roads and unsuspecting turn-offs amid all those great and wonderful destinations was the in-between. The wild places. The places not advertised on TV commercials or gigantic THANK YOU FOR VISITING billboards. Places without paved roads and gift shops and shuttle buses. Quiet, sacred places where the act of exploration was still a requirement. Places that were never supposed to be easy to find.

We versed ourselves in reading the topographic maps and guidebooks and mustered the courage to befriend the crusty gas station locals who smirked at our shiny pickup truck, our modern gear. But they welcomed our curiosity, our eagerness to stray. We were clued in to local secrets simply because we'd thought to ask.

In the midst of the thrill of discovering all these places was always the soul-sucking realization that we'd soon have to leave them. Whenever it was time to go, Dagwood would stand poised among the rabbit-brush, paws stained red with dirt, staring at us, bewildered as to why we'd ever take him from the desert.

It did seem criminal, almost. Like plucking a painting from the wall of a museum. We would bring him back to our studio apartment several hours north, where he would destroy everything in sight until we returned him to the red dirt the following weekend.

One Sunday afternoon, as autumn was slipping into winter, we drove down into our favorite canyon and parked the truck in one of the last remaining patches of sunlight. It wouldn't be long before we'd need to start the drive home. There was a constant longing for one more minute, one more sunset, one more whoosh of the cliff swallow's wings.

In no hurry, Neil cut up apple slices as I brushed sand and dog hair from the rim of a peanut butter jar. Bucket and Dagwood puttered about, sticking their noses into rodent burrows and beneath sandstone boulders, sending great puffs of sand out past both sides of their whiskers.

There, with our butts in the dirt and our faces in the sun, we dreamed aloud for the first time of never going back. It seemed we had both been thinking it, but were nervous to say it.

Would anyone notice, we wondered, if we simply disappeared among patches of sagebrush and pinyon pines? Would anyone care if our apartment was left vacant as our belongings gathered dust? Would we feel more at home if we had no home at all?

It sounded like a fever dream, and we both suspected that that was all it might ever be. After all, we were nearing our late twenties; our friends were buying homes and having babies and getting promotions and putting down roots. To sit in the sand and dream of running away? It seemed absurd, childish even.

We couldn't run away to the desert because that's just not what adults do. Adults pack their crazy dreams away, perhaps forever, or perhaps to push upon the next generation, who, for some unknown reason, might have a better shot at them than they did. Then they put on their ties and pay their mortgages because, at some point, someone told them their dreams were no longer feasible. And they believed them.

PART II

And then there is the most dangerous risk of all—the risk of spending your life not doing what you want on the bet you can buy yourself the freedom to do it later.

—RANDY KOMISAR

When I was in the third grade, my father cut his finger off on a table saw. In a split second, his hand slipped, sending the blade straight through the knuckle of his left pointer finger. In the chaos of trying to get himself to the hospital, he hadn't the slightest idea where the finger had landed. A couple of guys who worked for him walked all over the yard looking, but they never found it. For years afterward, my mother, father, brother, and I would sit around the dinner table dreaming up grand theories of where Dad's missing finger ended up.

The neighbor's dog ate it.

A bird swooped in and fed it to its hatchlings.

Someone was using it to commit crimes without leaving their own prints.

In random moments of silence, my brother would shout, "Raise your hand if you have ten fingers!" Forks would clatter to their plates as our three arms shot straight up. My dad would shrug his shoulders and yell, "Nine and a half!"

His favorite bit was to pull up to whatever social event he was picking me up from with that nub of a finger shoved up his nostril so it appeared he was knuckle-deep in his own brain. That was my dad. Always the comedian, always a bright light in the room. He came from a family of performers, which meant, of course, that I came from a family of performers. Oftentimes, you had to be entertaining just to get a word in.

His side of the family was a tossed-together collection of creatives. My grandfather was a painter, celebrated for his oil renderings of the marshes of Long Island Sound. My cousin became a model and Broadway actor, while another cousin managed one of the top symphony orchestras in the country. My aunt was an event planner; my uncle, the owner of a television studio. Another uncle was the face of a popular video game franchise and had been married to a famous actress from Japan. Their daughter became an abstract artist whose vast murals cover half of the buildings in her city. My own father spent his sixtieth birthday performing with his band, shimmying around a dance hall in his snakeskin cowboy boots.

If we had a family crest, it would likely be a paintbrush and a microphone crossed like two swords, accompanied by the words: *Look at Me!* But depression, addiction, and suicide were a part of our stories as well; the more unspoken, unfortunate hallmark of those who can't help but base the value of their existence on whether or not it is seen as beautiful or worthwhile.

Performance is how I feel love. It is also how I show love. As a little girl, my father would cup my cheeks in his calloused hands and say,

"My darling, you've got that *je ne sais quoi*"—French for a special something, literally translating to *I don't know what.* He said it with such sincerity, it was impossible to believe it wasn't true.

While much smaller in number, my mother's side of the family had their own complex history. My grandmother didn't really know how to show my mother love, because she didn't know love herself. Her mother—my great-grandmother—gave her up for adoption as a toddler and, despite living in the same town, never went looking for her again.

At sixteen, my grandmother became pregnant herself and was sent to live in a Catholic home for unwed mothers. She birthed a baby boy, delivered directly into the arms of a group of nuns who placed him up for adoption. My mother is still looking for her long-lost older brother to this day.

Several years later, my grandmother joined a convent to become a nun herself, before leaving abruptly to marry a man who would end up walking out on both her and their only child—my mother.

Decades later, after having a second daughter with another man, she finally found the courage to tell everyone what had truly tortured her all those years. She was gay. She'd known it for as long as she could remember.

I was sympathetic to my grandmother for the unimaginable burden she carried most of her life, but the long-kept secret was little comfort to my mother, who had endured an entire childhood in which *she* felt like a burden. No one had ever cupped her face and told her she was special.

After my grandmother revealed this truth, she had no qualms about making up for lost time. She threw out all her bras and spent her evenings dancing with her transgender friends at a bar called the Brook. Having been open for seventy-one years, it was considered one of the oldest gay bars in the nation. I imagined my grandmother driving past it for fifty years before finally throwing open the front doors and walking in.

It's been a long-standing joke that I was birthed into the world carrying the wrath of the women before me who were seldom allowed to be who they truly were; who were punished and guilted and shamed into silence. My mother nurtured this in me, ensuring there would be no more shrinking violets in the family. For my fifteenth birthday, she gifted me a T-shirt with the word *Chutzpah* emblazoned across the chest, an old Yiddish word that translates to "shameless audacity."

And so, I grew up believing that there weren't even any words in the English language to describe me. Quite the weight to bear as a kid, and quite a burden to live up to as an adult. As a teenager, I struggled to channel that fiery, self-righteous energy into anything overtly productive. Mostly I was just brash and defiant for the sake of being brash and defiant.

One summer day after my freshman year of high school, a letter came in the mail. My mother thrust it into my hands after reading it several times herself. The private Catholic school my parents worked so hard to send me to had kicked me out. It wasn't that I was skipping class or flunking tests. The letter simply said, *Brianna is a disruption.*

My mother called the school and begged to come in for a meeting.

In the heavy silence of a hot July day, we drove up and sat in front of the principal, the dean, and one of the nuns. I stared straight down at the desk as they explained how I repeatedly disregarded rules surrounding the uniform dress code, that I interrupted religion classes to defend birth control and gay marriage, that I was performative and combative and bull-headed. One of my yellow detention slips from the spring semester read: *Calling Jesus an asshole.*

My mother sat, stone-faced, listening to all the things she already knew to be true, but still she begged them to give me another chance.

Weeks later, another letter came in the mail containing the strict probation conditions under which I could return to school. Out of desperation, we agreed, and I did my best to keep my head down for the remainder of my enrollment, though I can't say I was too successful.

Three years later, my mother bought a page in the back of the yearbook, as was customary for graduating seniors. On it, she put funny baby photos and well wishes, but tucked inconspicuously throughout the page were little quotes from Mark Twain about the absurdity of uniforms and the danger of blind obedience, and Laurel Thatcher Ulrich's famous "Well-behaved women seldom make history."

My mother's final parting jab.

The messages my mother sent to me throughout my childhood were confusing sometimes. She was torn between the two places it seemed she had always been—respectable and rebellious—and it translated directly into the way she raised me. I suspect she always knew I would choose the latter, but her encouragement toward it was subtle. Funny T-shirts and words hidden in a yearbook page; bread crumbs leading me toward a trail I believe she often wished she took. Even in those moments when our eyes were downcast, being scolded by some shadowy woman in a nun's habit—a recurring theme for the women in my family, I suppose—I could feel her implied defiance. As if she were sitting there with her fingers crossed coyly behind her back. She knew there was a time and place where rules must be followed, because as soon as they turn their backs, you could begin to make your own.

The wedding dress I wore at the tender young age of twenty-four was champagne-pink, with a sweetheart neckline and a flower crown on my head so large one might have mistaken it for an Easter wreath. I chose the dress not because I particularly loved the color, but because it was the only thing *with* color. Standing in front of rack after rack of stark white and ivory gowns, it stuck out immediately and for that reason alone seemed like the logical choice.

Most of the decisions I've made in my life are products of this formula, of the curiously deep-seated need to be *against*. The scenario rarely mattered. If it was meant to be done one way, I was compelled to do it the other. It came so naturally to me in my younger years that I was convinced it would serve as a lifelong first instinct, a muscle memory as natural as blinking or breathing.

I thought about this one morning as I stared dull-eyed over the steering wheel on my way to work. I was twenty-six, making good money as a technical writer for a software company. My days were spent writing bone-dry instruction manuals for various clients and then complaining about those clients in the break room. If individuality came as naturally as breathing—as I had so arrogantly expected—I'd have surely suffocated by then.

It was humbling to realize how easily I had slipped into the kind of life I swore I'd never have. Despite how bitter I'd been growing up, the comfort of monotony cradled me in its arms and lulled me into a semi-conscious state of contentedness. The kind I might have been shocked to wake up from decades down the road, wondering where all that time went.

I left my office early one afternoon to meet Neil at a Chase Bank a few blocks over. Outside in the parking lot, he straightened the collar of his shirt in the reflection of his truck window. We walked in, hand in hand, and probably a little too loudly announced that we were there to speak to someone about a mortgage. A mortgage! A collared shirt! What great big, grown-up things!

We were itching for a change, for some kind of interruption from our relatively unremarkable day-to-day lives. It gave me something to look forward to. In between emails and board meetings, I'd spend hours on the internet looking at perfectly distressed leather couches and patio furniture and blogs about which gray paint color is the most soothing for bathrooms. It was something new, something different. That day at the bank, it felt like our next adventure was about to begin.

. . .

After a short wait, a nice man with a red tie came out and ushered us into his office. "How exciting!" he exclaimed, peering into our terror-stricken faces.

With a couple of questions and clicks, he pulled up our bank accounts and credit histories and began slinging terms like *APR* and *PMI* and *fixed rates* and *loan-to-value ratio* across the desk at us. He systematically laid out the next fifty years of our lives right there in front of us in numbers and words we didn't understand.

I sat there, nodding slowly and methodically, pretending to absorb the information, but the room was getting small. The man with the tie seemed farther away suddenly. It sounded like there was cotton in my ears. But then the narrowing vision and muffled voices gave way to the sound of something else. Wind. Seagulls. The clanging of metal against masts. *Satisfaction.* I could taste the salt. I could see the waves melting into silver at sunset; Neil leaping barefoot from rope to rope, tightening one and loosening the other as sea spray rained down over his bare back.

It felt a bit like standing at the altar and having an image of an old lover pop into your head. Did it mean something? Was it just a nervous brain's coping mechanism? Did I want a mortgage? Did I want any of this?

Neil gently squeezed my hand, pulling me back to reality, back to the bank. It was freezing in there.

"Why don't I give you two my card, and you can call me with any questions," the man suggested. "I'll be here when you're ready."

Back in the parking lot I stood next to the truck, staring blankly at the pavement, kicking my shoe against the tire like an angsty teenager who'd just failed a test.

"Maybe I don't want a fucking house!" I said.

Neil retaliated by reminding me that this was sort of my idea in the first place, that no one had actually told me I needed to buy one. And yet, oddly, it felt like someone had. It felt like I was failing somehow because I didn't have a tulip garden and a thirty-year fixed mortgage to go along with my office gig. This was supposed to be our next great adventure, but this didn't feel like an adventure at all. This felt . . . methodical. Like we were moving along some sort of human conveyor belt.

I lay in bed that night staring up at the ceiling of our basement apartment. At what point had I stopped paying attention? At what point had I begun assuming that some defiant portion of my personality was going to be enough to land me in a life I wanted? I had always been comfortable going against the grain, but the older I got, the more effort it seemed it would require.

My life was not destined to be an exciting one simply because I rolled my eyes at "normality." I was going to have to consciously decide to swim upstream day after day, like a mixed-up migratory fish, until I reached whatever destination was instinctually gnawing at my bones. I thought to myself, *The next time I go into that bank, I'll be prepared.*

Unbeknownst to me in that moment, the next time I would go into that bank was exactly seven days later.

The morning after our mortgage meeting, a text message from Neil lit up my phone as it sat on my desk at work. It was a photo of a classified ad in which someone from North Salt Lake was selling a bright-orange behemoth of a Ford van for $7,800. It had four-wheel drive and the bare bones of a bed frame built out in the back where the seats had once been.

I stared at the picture for what felt like an hour with my thumbs hovering over the keyboard until something made them start to move.

"Get it," I wrote.

When he didn't immediately reply, I picked up the phone and called him.

"Let's do it, let's get it," I said, feverishly.

Neil was so caught off guard by my reaction that all he could muster was laughter. But I felt a sudden sense of urgency. This was our chance. This was our out. What I saw in that photo was a getaway car.

"Seriously, Neil, let's do it," I said, in an even voice now.

He paused and I held my breath in the silence.

"Really?" he asked.

"Yes, I'm going to call right now," I replied, practically hanging up on him.

I stood from my desk and walked out into the parking lot of my office building. Hands trembling in the February air, I punched in the phone number listed on the ad.

After a few rings, a man's voice answered, and it was only in that moment that I realized what I was actually doing.

"Hi, um, I'm calling about the orange van?" I stuttered.

"Yes?" he said, hurriedly.

"Is it, um . . . is it available?" I asked, feeling slightly ridiculous now.

"Yea, I got two people comin' to look at it tomorrow, when can you come by?" he replied.

My heart sank as I explained that my husband wouldn't be back from work until Saturday and I didn't think I was at all qualified to go up there alone.

His voice softened.

"Listen," he said, "why don't you call me on Saturday and I'll let you know if it's still here."

I thanked him and hung up, and then I sat on a curb in the parking lot for a good long while. It seemed impossible that a listing like that would be around almost a full week from then, so I tried not to get too attached. But that fleeting glimpse, that flash of a life that could be had swept me up like a storm. As I walked back to my office, the lights seemed duller. Everything looked white and gray, monotone and drab. All I could see now was orange.

Neil seemed surprised that my fascination with the van hadn't waned by the time he got back from his shift. He walked into our basement apartment and heaved his backpacks onto the floor as the dogs tackled him. He always smelled like juniper smoke, his skin veiled over with desert dirt. I watched him from across the room, fidgeting with the buttons on my phone.

"It's still there, Neil," I said quietly. "I called the guy again this morning and no one has put an offer down yet."

His eyes met mine, upside down from where he lay on the living room rug scratching Bucket's velvet ears, and he smiled.

We drove north on the freeway toward the parking lot the man from the ad told us to meet him in. Neil lectured me on the fact that it was an old van; it probably had rust, it probably had all kinds of mechanical problems. But I was busy staring out the window at the cookie-cutter houses carved into the foothills. Brown stucco with brown roofs and brown shutters, smashed up against one another row after row after row.

We turned slowly down side streets where empty warehouses loomed in weekend silence. In the corner spot of the last one on the left, a colossal orange rectangle. The van was so huge in person, it was practically cartoonish. Neil's pickup truck was dwarfed in its shadow. We walked circles around it as we waited for the seller to appear.

The front end was snub-nosed and square, retro-looking in a way. The tires were about as high as my waist, and the orange paint job had clearly been a DIY project, as glossy drip marks dotted the exterior. Neil had climbed underneath to check for rust when a door to the warehouse swung open. A bearded guy walked out and introduced himself as Joe. He and Neil began talking details about mileage and repair and owner history.

I opened the driver's side door to the faded blue interior, peeling at the bottom corners of the door panel. It reminded me of my grandmother's old station wagon. The steering wheel and its entire steering column sagged downward toward me as I stood in the doorway. Joe explained that years of previous owners reaching up and using the wheel to hoist themselves into the driver's seat were the culprit of that signature sag. She was just *that* big.

He tossed us the keys and told us to take her around the block. Neil fired it up and I pulled myself into the passenger seat. It felt like being at the helm of a school bus. We drove slowly down the street, hardly able to hear each other over the 7.5-liter engine, though I can't remember exactly what it was we were saying anyway.

Somewhere beneath the deafening hum of tires and the smell of dusty brakes, we had made up our minds. The idea of the two of us rolling around in this outlandish orange van made more sense than anything we had considered prior. This was our getaway car from a life of supposed-tos and should-haves.

But if the potential of a mortgage had felt like dipping our toe into the big, daunting pool of life, then buying this van would be like careening off the high dive. And yet, bizarrely enough, that felt safer.

• • •

When we arrived back in the parking lot where Joe stood, Neil pulled his wallet from the back pocket of his jeans. Sheepishly, he explained that we would need to wait until the following week for another paycheck to come through so that we could take out the full asking price of $7,800 in cash. At that moment, we only had about $7,000 in savings. We offered up the hundred or so we had on us if he would just hold the van until then. Joe leaned forward and plucked one single twenty-dollar bill from the crinkled fan of money in Neil's hand.

"Don't worry, I won't sell it on ya." He smiled.

The following Friday, after Neil's paycheck had cleared, I left my office to drive back to the bank. I strode in more assuredly this time, past the ATMs, past the office of the man in the red tie, and up to the counter, where a clerk asked from behind the glass what she could do for me that morning.

"I need all my money," I answered back hurriedly, before realizing that that sounded a bit like the opening line to a robbery.

"I need to withdraw everything that I have in both checking and savings," I said again, slower this time.

I was expecting some sort of grandiose reaction from the handful of tellers behind the long glass window. I wanted everyone in that bank to understand that I was standing here doing the most insane thing I'd ever done. But in reality, I was just another person withdrawing a totally unimpressive amount of cash, and for what, they really didn't care.

Despite the change in tone I'd made inside the bank, I still left feeling like I had robbed the place. I sat in the driver's seat of my

Jeep and opened the white envelope full of cash. More cash than I'd ever seen. All the cash we had to our names. In fact, the balance in our checking account was zero, and the balance in our savings was about seventeen dollars. I was twenty-six years old and I had seventeen dollars.

We drove up that evening to make the exchange. I had no interest in carrying that amount of money on me any longer than I needed to. Once back in the warehouse lot, we handed over the cash, and Joe handed over a two-inch-thick file. Meticulous records of every repair, every modification, every maintenance item that had been done to the van. So meticulous, in fact, that the very last piece of paper in the folder was the decal sticker that had been on the van's windshield on the lot in 1990. The same year that I was born.

Joe shook our hands and gave us the keys. It was the most official-seeming gesture throughout the entire process, and I was caught up in the excitement of it when I realized suddenly that Neil and Joe were both staring at me expectantly. It hadn't quite occurred to me that I would be the one to drive this van back to our apartment forty-five minutes south. We had come up in Neil's pickup truck, a stick shift Toyota that I had never properly learned to drive. I feigned confidence—something I would become an expert at in the coming months—and climbed into the driver's seat alone.

I'd always considered myself a good driver. When I was a child, my dad would prop me up in his lap in the driver's seat of his work van.

He would push the pedals and I would turn the wheel, enveloped in the sawdust scent of his flannel shirtsleeves. He'd play the Grateful Dead's "Friend of the Devil" over and over until the lyrics settled permanently into my six-year-old brain. I'd sing them back to him, methodically. *Got a wife in Chino, babe, and one in Cherokee, first one say she got my child, but it don't look like me.*

My mother, on the other hand, sick to death of driving me around, began letting me take her car at age fourteen so long as I promised not to cross over a street everyone referred to as "the Avenue."

I'd drive myself down to the waterfront, or the ice cream shop, or the corner market to get an egg sandwich. One morning, the owner of that market called my mother to say he'd seen me driving around the neighborhood. He knew for certain I was not even old enough to apply for a learner's permit, let alone have a license. My mother feigned shock at the news, and that was the end of my joyriding.

By the time I *actually* got my license, I was completely at home behind the wheel. Parallel parking was practically a hobby of mine, and rush-hour traffic out of New York City didn't faze me in the slightest. A decade later, behind the wheel of that van, I'd never felt more inept.

I lumbered out of the parking lot, suspecting every slight adjustment of the wheel might topple the whole thing over. The smallest breeze shifted me to whichever side of the road it pleased.

I merged slowly onto the freeway and into evening traffic. Inching forward through tightly packed lanes, I realized I couldn't see the faces of the drivers in passing sedans. I was so high up, I could only look down at their legs. I was now making eye contact with the drivers of passing tractor trailers instead.

In a sudden and sobering moment of clarity, it occurred to me what I had done. Like waking up from sleepwalking to find yourself standing in the kitchen, I came to and realized I was holding the steering wheel of a van I'd bought on a whim. What was the plan? Where was I? Better yet, who was I? In a matter of one week, I had gone from looking at floor plans and mortgages to riding eye-level with truckers with seventeen dollars left to my name. And yet, part of me was thrilled at the absurdity of it all.

Somewhere deep in my gut, I'd known that my quest to "settle down" was a sham. I was just playing a role I'd seen; doing things because it seemed like I was supposed to, not because I actually wanted to. I'd toddled into that mortgage loan meeting like a child in her mother's high heels, clumsy and clueless.

Being behind the wheel of that van felt honest. Perhaps because uncertainty felt more like home than anything else.

Upon my safely arriving back at our basement apartment, Neil ran inside to fetch the dogs as I opened the van's sliding door in preparation. Dagwood came bounding across the gravel and took one flying leap from the sidewalk into the van as though he'd been waiting his whole life for that thing to pull up. Bucket followed closely behind, skidding to a halt on the sidewalk before peering at me inquisitively. She was hesitant—a quality she'd never lost from puppyhood—so I had to lift all sixty-five pounds of her up and in to join her brother.

"Where should we go?" Neil asked, climbing into the driver's seat. The dogs were already fogging up the windows with their breath.

"Anywhere!" I exclaimed, bouncing in my seat. Neil nodded enthusiastically as he cranked the key in the ignition.

Nothing.

He tried it again. Still nothing.

We sat there, dumbfounded, as the realization washed over us. Were we those sorry saps people read about in the local news? The idiots who got swindled into giving away their every penny for a big, hulking pile of crap?

I let out a slew of expletives as Neil jumped back out and popped the hood. He clanked around under there as a cold sweat formed on my forehead. How the fuck was I going to tell my mother that we'd given away all of our savings for a vehicle that stopped working the moment we took it home? Just before I spiraled into complete panic, Neil's head popped out from the side of the open hood.

"The battery lines are corroded," he smiled, nervously, "that's all!"

I had no idea what that actually meant but yelled, "Oh good!" in return.

Neil had always been that way. Not so much a handyman as a savant, taking one look at the wiry guts of a vehicle or a washing machine or a bicycle and immediately understanding the inner workings.

He drove his truck over to an auto parts shop to get the necessary replacement parts and had her up and running again in under an hour. We drove that van all over Salt Lake City that night, picking up friends from their various apartments, piling them into our little orange school bus, blasting our music with all the windows down. We were ecstatic and clueless and terrified and free.

We named her Bertha after the Grateful Dead song. *I was all night running, running, running.* She was windows all the way around, but they had a dark tint over them, making it quite cave-like. A carpeted platform with thin metal legs covered the majority of the rear, designed to serve as a place for a mattress. A bench seat that originally faced forward had been turned sideways to face the sliding side door like a couch. Before it was a small open floor space covered in corkboard and then linoleum and then one single melted gummy worm from the prior owner's kid.

I sewed some window curtains cut from an old tapestry and strung prayer flags up across the windshield. Some friends gifted us a futon mattress from IKEA that was thick enough to be comfortable but thin enough to not add extra height to the bed frame. When we sat up on it, our heads were perfectly flush against the fabric-lined ceiling.

The rear double doors opened to a large compartment under the bed where we kept our camp chairs, an old Coleman stove, a few plastic bins for food and dishware, four five-gallon blue jugs for water, and a cooler that we would sometimes remember to put ice in.

She was bare bones in the grand scheme of the fancy Sprinter vans and RVs with marble countertops, but to us, she was pure luxury. The dogs loved the van so much, we had to coax them out of it, practically dragging them across the sidewalk toward our apartment each time. Dagwood would often escape the small fenced-in yard behind our place and tiptoe down the driveway toward the van. We would peer out the window and catch him out there, fast asleep up against one of the massive black tires. If that van moved, he was going with it.

Our weekend adventures continued on religiously, packing the van up every Friday with boxes of mac and cheese and beer instead of

Neil's truck. A position change within his company meant that Neil now had three days on per week and four days off. Saturday, Sunday, Monday, and Tuesday were his to go wherever he pleased.

I begged my own boss to let me work remotely on Mondays and Tuesdays, convincing him that I was calling in from my apartment down the street, when really I was standing on top of Bertha in the middle of a desert canyon with my arm outstretched toward the sky, trying desperately to get enough service to send a single email.

It was irresponsible, sure, but so was draining your entire bank account on a van. We were now the kind of people who bailed on work, who white-lied our way into weekly adventures without thinking twice. The moment I climbed up into Bertha, I was free to be as outrageous as she was.

I wish I could tell you we spent months building the van out and meticulously planning our move into it, but the decision to live in the van full-time was almost as manic as the decision to buy it in the first place.

By August 2016, we had begun referring to our apartment as "the gear room." A place we'd swing by occasionally to unload one backpack and repack another. A place that felt more like a garage or a toolshed than anything else, except it was a toolshed that was costing us $850 a month.

We had talked about living in the van hundreds of times, teetering on the edge of all the what-ifs and unknowns. How would we store food? How would we keep two dogs alive in a van? How would we keep our jobs? Where would we get mail? Where would we shower? What would our parents say?

And yet, without a single answer to any of those questions, we broke the lease on our apartment, packed a few backpacks, shoved some furniture and a box of kitchen supplies into a storage unit, dumped the rest off at Goodwill, and drove the van down to the city park around the corner from our apartment.

"Our *old* apartment," I corrected Neil, with a smile.

It was yet another reminder that most pivotal moments in our lives usually come without the pomp and circumstance we imagine. There was no parade. No one came to wave us off. We simply traded a set of four walls for a set of four wheels on a Tuesday afternoon in September and the world spun on.

In retrospect, I'm glad I didn't spend months researching the ins and outs of the decision we were about to make. I learned almost immediately that there were no shortcuts to living in a van. Figuring it out *was* the point. That's what made it different. The answer to most every question, most every dilemma, was simple, and it was probably right in front of me. Over time, my brain had learned to obscure the obvious in favor of the complicated. So much stood to be unlearned.

The first dilemma was my job. I was still employed full-time, so one of the first orders of business would be to inform the human resources department that I no longer had an address and would occasionally be sleeping in the parking lot. As one might imagine, the head of employee relations sat across from me in a gray suit jacket, dumbfounded.

I confidently laid out the terms of my new arrangements while hiding my shaking hands on my lap beneath the table. I would need to continue working remotely for half the week. I would need to be moved from a cubicle to my own private office so that I could bring my dogs to work without disturbing anyone. I would need to keep a small supply of toiletries in the downstairs bathroom. I would need building security staff to be made aware that they might see me wandering the parking lot in my pajamas.

My hands had stopped shaking by the time I finished, believing it wasn't all as crazy as it sounded when I had rehearsed it in my head, but I was met with the exact same dumbfounded face. She held a finger up, rose silently, and left the room, returning several minutes later with my boss—a native San Franciscan who split his time between Utah and California. His reaction was less dumbfounded and more amused. To my surprise, he agreed to all the terms under the sole condition that my work ethic didn't suffer.

"We'll give it a trial period," he said with a wink, before casually walking back out the door.

"I suppose I'll have IT start setting up one of the empty offices downstairs," the still-bewildered woman said.

My nine-to-five job was practically a comedic contrast to the other parts of my life. I started out as an account manager but graduated to technical writer when the CEO found out I had a BA in writing and rhetoric and shouted, "You're the new technical writer!" across the bar at happy hour.

It was a bizarre little software company—founded and still operated by an aging millionaire with a name like something from *The Great Gatsby*. People were constantly being hired and fired and sometimes *re*hired . . . and then refired. The account managers were always chasing down the project managers, who had to chase down the sales team, who were probably loitering in the employee kitchen.

It was a tumultuous, unpredictable place to work, but people stuck around for as long as they could possibly bear because of the rousing happy hours, the free daily catered lunch, and the positively nonchalant nature of the office itself.

Employees came and went as they pleased, took six weeks of vacation per year, worked from home without asking. I shouldn't have been as surprised as I was when they agreed to let me live in a van and shower in their men's room. I was very surprised, however, that they allowed me to bring Bucket and Dagwood with me each day.

At approximately 7:30 a.m. we would come bursting through the office doors, me and two half-snow-covered hounds at my heel. I'd point my finger and cluck them toward the stairs, and sometimes they would listen but most times they'd round the corner and head for the desk of the woman who stole bits of chicken from the kitchen for them.

Often, I'd be hauling a frozen five-gallon water jug that I would thaw in front of my space heater throughout the day in order to have drinking water for the upcoming night. At first glance, one might think I had broken into the place, but each day I ushered my little circus down the stairs and around the corner into my very own office.

My coworkers were pretty divided on the topic of my presence in general. Most of the IT department were nervous around the dogs, and with its being a largely Mormon-run company, I can't say too many folks were comfortable with me showering in the basement either. Even beyond the whole nudity aspect, there *was* something understandably uncomfortable about making eye contact with a coworker with wet hair and a toothbrush hanging from your mouth.

On the other hand, a lot of folks got a kick out of it all, gathering around my office door to ask what exciting adventures the old orange van had gotten into that weekend. I attempted to keep a low profile, but low profiles were never my strong suit. Eventually, I grew to simply embrace the comedic aspect of it all. I was the company-appointed court jester.

One morning, a gentleman from the sales team asked to take a peek inside Bertha. He was fascinated with how I was "living in this thing." So, I gave him the shockingly short tour. Here is the bed and here is the couch and here are some drawers and a cooler.

I explained that we didn't quite live *in* the van so much as we lived *out* of the van. The "kitchen" was nothing more than a Coleman stove, a foldable table, plastic bins of food, and a few pots and pans. We were essentially camping every day of our lives.

A string of old Christmas lights taped around the inside circumference was the easiest thing we could come up with for lighting. They were powered by a slightly damaged solar panel on the roof that Neil found in the local classified ads.

In many of the newer vans like the Sprinter, tall walls, decent headspace, and lack of windows made for an easy install of insulation. But trying to live inside a 1990 Ford with a body that is 50 percent glass windows made attempts at insulation futile.

I left Home Depot one day after work with two rolls of silver Reflectix under each arm and spent the afternoon right there in the parking lot cutting it to fit the shape of each window. As the autumn sun dipped lower, I would take breaks to blow warm breath onto my fingertips, battling the sheets of glorified Bubble Wrap.

By the time I finished, the van looked like the inside of a tuna can and was probably a whole four degrees warmer. But for what it lacked in temperature regulation, it made up for in privacy. With the windshield cover up, the van was almost completely blacked out. Passersby might never even suspect anyone was in there.

That hope proved false a few weeks later when a large fist rapped on our driver's side window at three o'clock in the morning.

"You got a boot on!" a man's voice shouted over Bucket's and Dagwood's frenzied barking. Half-asleep and completely disoriented, Neil shouted back, "What?!"

"You got a boot!" another voice yelled through the passenger window. It appeared we were surrounded.

Neil clambered, shirtless, up to the front seat as I searched frantically in the dark for my headlamp. I calmed the dogs and slid the side door open, where I was met with the flashing lights of a purple tow truck in the vacant parking lot we had settled on sleeping in that night.

It took me a solid minute or so to realize that *they* had put the boot on our van. They knew we were asleep inside and instead of simply waking us up and telling us to leave, they slapped a boot on our tire and were now demanding eighty dollars in cash to take it off.

"What the fuck?!" I shouted at one of the men, who had to be at least six feet tall and four hundred pounds.

"Can't park here," he mumbled before rocketing a wad of dip spit onto the pavement beside him.

"There's no signs *anywhere* that say that!" I protested.

That's when the other portly gentleman rounded the back corner of the van with Neil behind him and casually mentioned, "There's a little sign down on the first level of the parking garage at one of the entrances on Third West."

Neil and I stared blankly at him, then each other, and then back at him.

"There's . . . one sign? There's one fucking sign?!"

Bucket and Dagwood howled from inside the van.

"M-hmm," mumbled the first guy, ". . . can't park here."

"Yeah, I heard you the first time, asshole," I snarled.

The other man offered to give Neil a ride to an ATM to retrieve the cash we were being forced to hand over. He climbed barefoot into the passenger seat of the neon tow truck and headed off toward the nearest bank. I can only imagine what small talk they made on the way.

I stayed behind, leaning up against the van with arms crossed, staring down the big fella as he packed a fresh lip. He smirked at me, and in retrospect, I have to imagine that being called an asshole by a woman in a parking lot wearing pajamas is a pretty mild encounter for someone in his line of work.

A short while later, Neil returned with the eighty bucks. With a click and a snap, the boot was removed and we were free to roll on in search of a new place to post up until sunrise.

Since I was still spending half the week at my office, finding places to stealth camp around Salt Lake City was more a part of my routine than cliffside campsites and desert horizons. The parking lot outside my office building proved quite the late-night stomping ground for dumpster divers and the occasional exchange of services that usually take place exclusively under streetlights. We had an extensive local community of friends, but most of them were dirtbags like us. They could hardly afford the apartments they were crammed into, let alone the kind of place that had a flat driveway for me to park in.

Neil was still away at work several days a week, so the task of hiding throughout the city was often mine and mine alone. I resorted to a rotating cycle of suburban streets throughout the city. My favorite was just down the hill from our best friends' place in front of a small apartment complex beneath a streetlight that was dimmer than most. It was dark and flat and quiet and with all those apartments there, I figured neighbors would just assume I was visiting some other neighbor.

Another favorite of mine was outside of a day care, which, in retrospect, is tremendously creepy. In my defense, it was always pitch-black after hours and I tried to be awake and out of there before any children arrived. No matter where I was parked, nothing made me feel more criminal than holding my breath inside a van as children passed by outside, unaware.

One morning on his off-shift, Neil slid the van door open on a side street near the dog park in nothing but boxers just in time to make eye contact with a mother and her young son passing by on the sidewalk. Needless to say, we never slept over there again.

But despite the few mishaps with tow trucks and terrified parents, I had become pretty good at city camping. I'd dip into gas stations or grocery stores, use the bathrooms to brush my teeth or splash water on my face, then slink back out to the van and stumble over the dogs as I slipped into my long johns in a combined floor space the size of a refrigerator.

Once ready for bed, I'd drive over to the spot of my choosing, shut the engine off, put the windshield cover up, and immediately climb under the covers. If I planned to sleep in front of a stranger's house, I couldn't be cracking the doors open, turning all the lights on, and brushing my teeth outside their dining room window. I had to look like every other parked car on the street. Except . . . oranger.

I suppose it was hilariously futile to think I was blending in at all in a massive orange van with thirty-three-inch tires and a homemade shower, roof box, bike rack, and solar panel strapped to it. Parked between Toyota Camrys and Volkswagen Jettas, I looked like something out of a Mad Max movie.

In some way, I thought it might play to my favor that Bertha looked more like an adventure-mobile as opposed to a kidnap-your-child-mobile. But even if folks thought I was some cool rock climber, they still didn't want me camping on their front lawn.

It all felt a bit like being on the run. From what, I wasn't quite certain. Despite the fact that I was so proud of this funny little home we'd made, it still felt like a secret that begged to be kept. Don't let them see the lights on! Don't let them hear! Don't let them catch us!

My life in the desert on the weekends was freedom. It was walking naked through the sand and sleeping with all the doors wide open and showering with handfuls of muddy river water that didn't belong to anyone in particular.

But my life in the city was like a grown-up game of hide-and-seek. Constantly concealing. Constantly tiptoeing. Constantly giggling at the terrifying and thrilling notion of being found.

In this game, I came to understand the nuances of what was illegal and what was just socially unacceptable. For example, it isn't *illegal* to cook grilled cheese sandwiches on a camp stove in a supermarket parking lot, but people will stare at you as though it is. It isn't *illegal* to use the shower on the roof of your van to wash your armpits at a public park in the middle of the day, but people will relocate their family picnics pretty quickly. It isn't *illegal* to dump plastic Gatorade bottles filled with a night's worth of urine into a toilet at a gas station, but it's probably best to not get caught carrying it in there in the first place.

Yes, most of the time, people couldn't quite put their finger on what exactly it was that I was doing wrong. Even the occasional law enforcement officer struggled to scold me. "I'd give you a ticket," a security guard once said, ". . . but I don't even know what I'd write on it."

And yet, where the law fell short, societal implications held strong. There seemed to be a broad understanding that I was failing to comply with the guidelines of a civilized world. Even children, in all their innocence, would stare mystified as I sat cross-legged in pavement parking lots, washing my hair in a metal dog bowl or hanging clothes out to dry on my passenger door.

I was breaking the rules. Rules we all learned before we even realized we were learning them.

The honeymoon phase of our life in the van came to an abrupt end with the first snowfall. Our faces were still sun-flushed from a weekend in the desert, but as Bertha puttered north toward Salt Lake City, I watched as golden fields disappeared beneath falling snow. It was the first time we had driven with the windows rolled up since the day we moved into the van.

A panic swept over us as freezing wind pierced the cracked rubber door seals of a twenty-seven-year-old tin can rolling along at sixty-five miles per hour. We were so caught up in long, hot desert days, baths in the muddy Colorado, and nights spent sleeping with every door wide open that we had forgotten how summer slips into fall and then slides violently into winter.

I was grateful to still have my office job simply for the fact that it was a warm place to go. Sleeping in a van in the cold is the easy part. Finding something to do until it's time to bury yourself beneath a dozen blankets was a lot harder. Plenty of friends offered up their warm couches, but many nights, I was too stubborn.

I'm not sure what I was trying to prove, or who I was trying to prove it to, but sleeping inside felt like cheating. Here I was, living in a van, breaking free of society's rules, and yet here I was building my own set of imaginary rules to fill the void.

You *have* to sleep outside, otherwise you don't truly live in a van! You *have* to wear the same pair of pants for six days in a row, otherwise you don't truly live in a van! Much of the "vanlife" Instagram pages and hashtags were just people bickering over who was breaking the rules right. We humans are absolutely brilliant at getting in our own way.

And so, my stubborn winter routine was such that each morning—whether alone or with Neil, whether in the desert or in the city—I woke to the sight of my breath. The interior of Bertha's windows were luminescent sheets of ice; the frozen condensation of two humans and two dogs breathing warm air into the cold night. I would lean forward from our mess of sleeping bags and blankets and dog hair and slide open the wooden drawer Neil built for my clothes. I'd pick a pair of jeans and a long-sleeve shirt and bury them down by my feet beneath the blankets in an attempt to warm them.

I lived in a van that was regularly covered in snow, so people assumed *I* was cold, but very few paused to consider that all my stuff was cold too. My jeans were frozen. My toothpaste was frozen. My face cream was frozen. There was nothing but a thin sheet of metal between me and the outside world, and at no time was I more aware of that than a winter morning.

I'd fire up the engine and use an expired credit card to scrape the ice from the inside of the windshield. It would fall like snow cone shavings onto the dash and melt down into the vents as Bertha's engine sputtered and fought for heat.

Bucket and Dagwood remained firmly curled at the base of the sleeping bags long after I had climbed out to face the day. Their bodies emanated heat and kept our toes from going numb night after night. We had tried a variety of tricks we thought might work to keep us all from freezing to death, including an old dirtbag trick of peeing into a bottle and shoving it down to the bottom of your bag. But our shared body heat always seemed to be the most reliable.

The four of us would slither into a double-person sleeping bag, two people and two fifty-plus-pound dogs mashed together. Sometimes I would attempt to read a book, struggling to turn the pages through my wool mittens. Some nights, the temperature would get so low, our electronics would shut off unexpectedly while we scrolled through social media or in the middle of a Netflix episode we were watching with nearby stolen Wi-Fi. Most winter nights we were asleep by 7:00 p.m.

When Neil was down at work, when strange sounds outside the van still startled me, the dogs and I resorted to spending nights over in the upscale part of the city. Sleeping in front of the beautiful houses of strangers was comforting to me. I'd lie awake in the morning, scratching Bucket's head, staring up into the faded fabric that lined Bertha's ceiling, and I'd listen.

Children running out the door to catch the school bus and the family retriever being called back inside. Engines firing up in driveways and dads out shoveling snow. I got to experience the comfortable familiarity of suburban life without actually living it. I was a secret neighbor of sorts; inserting myself into daily routines, unbeknownst to the very people performing them. Sometimes I would daydream about climbing through their windows, slipping under warm blankets in front of their fireplaces. After all, there was still a little girl out there in that van who had lost all of that. In a way, hiding in an old van in the nice part of town was reminiscent of the way I'd felt for most of my life. Always on the cusp of acceptance, always teetering on the edge of belonging. A part of me still needed to feel close enough to peer through the glass.

Those streets made me think of my childhood home and the two towns it sat on the border of. I thought of my mother gingerly placing seashells in each window and burying two fledgling cherry trees in the front yard. She mowed our own grass religiously and then moved on to mowing all the neighbors' grass because she thought it made the street look nicer. Then she started pushing the mower down the sidewalk to the marsh-front at the end of the road and mowing that grass too.

My father tried to stop her from spending money on flowers that she intended to plant in the center median down on the main avenue, but she wouldn't hear it. She could be found down there, half-sitting in the road with her pink gardening gloves, replanting daffodils that the drunks would inevitably run over the following weekend.

The outside appearance of our life mattered deeply to her, but when all was said and done, those cherry trees were the only thing that stood the test of time. Thick and glossy in their trunks and slightly unruly in their branches, they rose strong from the soil in front of that little blue house long after we had left.

"They're not trimming them enough," my mother said quietly one afternoon when she and I decided to drive by the old place. The grief in her voice was palpable. I sat there staring at her, and she at the trees, as if at any moment she might leap from the car and run to them with a pair of shears. They were hers, after all. Most of the other things that had grown in that house were gone.

My parents divorced when I was sixteen, but I was only twelve when I heard my mother whisper things like "drugs" and "rehab" to my grandmother over the phone. She had told me to go to my room, but I stood with my ear pressed against the door, tracing white drips of dried paint with my finger.

I couldn't understand most of the mumbling, but I couldn't understand most of the things I heard clearly either. I pictured Officer Friendly standing in front of my grade school classroom, a projector screen proudly displaying the word *D.A.R.E.* across the chalkboard. To a twelve-year-old, drugs were something nefarious-looking teenagers did in the alleyway behind the school. Drugs were the reason people ended up living beneath highway overpasses, soaked in their own urine.

Drugs were not something my dad did. He was just goofy, a big kid at heart. He was my own Jim Carrey from my favorite Ace Ventura movies. All the voices and the accents and the silly faces. That's just who he was. That had to be who he was, because I couldn't fathom that some brown liquor was in his Coca-Cola cans. That some substance was pumping through the arms he used to spin me around in the swimming pool, making whirlpools with my little legs.

He left for rehab in the fall at a facility in Pennsylvania. "If anyone asks, he's on vacation," my mother instructed us, firmly. We drove up a few weeks later for a family weekend where I sat around with a bunch of other wide-eyed kids. It seemed as though we'd all been kidnapped. Robbed of the safety of being a clueless child.

Therapists talked to us all about drugs and alcohol and depression and addiction and all the horrible things they can do to your body and your mind.

I thought about the time my mother found a couple of beers and a bag of weed in my brother's closet. She poured them down the drain in front of him, one by one, then flushed the bag down the toilet, plastic and all. *It will rot your brain*, she said. *You'll drink and you'll get high and you won't remember a damn thing*, she said.

What if my dad's brain was rotten? I pictured the way he would lie in his zombie costume in the front yard inside a wooden coffin he built every Halloween. When kids got close enough to think it was safe, he'd pop up and send them screaming, wriggling with joy, off into the darkness. It was practically a neighborhood tradition.

Did he remember that? What if he didn't remember that? I wanted to jump up from the circle of kids sitting cross-legged on the floor. I wanted to run screaming through the building, calling out for him. I needed to know if he remembered being a zombie in the front yard.

But I didn't jump up from the circle. I stayed frozen on the floor as the therapists droned on. Perhaps I knew that, even if I found him, I wouldn't recognize him anymore. The shape of him would be there; the dark brown eyes, the deep, tanned skin, the calloused hands that had always made me feel so small, so safe. If I saw him now, those things would seem like nothing more than a costume. One look would send me running, screaming, like any other kid on Halloween who's just seen a monster.

My mom was diligent about therapy for my brother and I after my dad left for rehab, but no one in the family seemed to really want to sit down and explain much to me. Sure, I was young, but I wasn't that young. The whole process felt like something we were just trying to rush through before anyone else found out.

Despite rehab and therapy and attempts at sobriety, my parents began a trial separation a few months later. The little blue house was packed up in boxes, photos stripped from either side of the staircase. My cousins and me at the beach with our bright red buckets. My dad with his two brothers at a racetrack. My grandmother holding me just a few hours after I was born. I helped my mom stack them in a dark storage unit like a game of Tetris.

She and I moved into an apartment on the very last street that was technically considered part of the Black Rock neighborhood. Dad moved into an apartment in the heart of Bridgeport. A family that once lived smack-dab in the middle was now on separate sides. My brother stayed over with my dad most of the time, likely because it was easier to hide beer and weed in the closet.

I only went over there once. I remember my sunburnt teenage

legs sticking awkwardly to the cheap leather couch, but not much else. It was foreign and disorienting to see my dad there, in what looked like someone else's house. I never went back.

A year or so later, on a Friday night, some friends and I were driving along through Fairfield's wooded back roads when we got word of a pool party happening at the house of some kid whose parents weren't home.

They sat in the idling car outside my apartment while I ran in to grab a bathing suit. All the lights were off, so I was surprised when I heard hushed voices down the hall. Then, as I gently pulled my bedroom door closed to leave, I heard the distinct sound of my dad's voice.

The doorknob to my mom's bedroom was locked. I banged my fist against the wood. A few minutes later, they both emerged, tousled and flustered from doing something I was now certainly old enough to understand.

Perhaps I should have been happy about their reconciliation. God knows most kids still fall asleep dreaming they'll wake up to find Mom and Dad in the kitchen again. But I was livid, cursing and slamming doors, dishing out glares that could freeze hell over. It seemed, to me, that it had all been for nothing.

My childhood bedroom was in a box in a dimly lit storage unit. Some other adorable American family was living in my blue house, their shiny new bicycles tipped over sideways in my driveway. They had even kept my cat. My parents thought he was too old to leave the only place he'd lived his whole life. His arthritis couldn't manage a second-story apartment, and the new owners were happy to take him.

Sometimes I'd ride my bike by and see his yellow-green eyes looking out from beneath a rosebush that was still his, but no longer mine.

After weeks of giving them the silent treatment, I began to warm up to the idea of my mom and dad being my mom and dad again. Dad's big black pickup truck parked on the street. The ever-present pot of coffee he had prepared at all hours of the day and night. The sound of them laughing in the bathroom together. Mom would sit on his lap and pluck the dark hairs from between his eyebrows with her tweezers.

They were bringing the tiny, comforting parts of my childhood back. I suppose that's all that childhood is, really. Just a series of little things that feel safe. The glow of a lightning bug. The creaking of old springs on a trampoline. The name of the boy you kissed under the lunch table in second grade. Mom's perfume.

I was a little girl again in that apartment. My brother was in college across the country by then. It was just my mom and my dad and me and all the little things that felt familiar. I had been mourning the loss of the skin of the little blue house. What I was really missing were the bones.

It was Valentine's Day when my mother walked in on my father with the woman from the church choir. She had gone to the movies with my brother and left me at the apartment on the couch with my high school boyfriend. My dad said he had to work late.

After the movie, they stopped by to surprise him at one of his half-built houses. There were candles and roses and music, interrupted only by my mother's gasp and my brother's fist connecting squarely with the jaw of his own father.

My brother stormed off into the night, but my mom came straight home and collapsed at the bottom of the staircase that led to our apartment. She screamed my name in a breathless, panicked kind of way. I flew down to where she lay, crumpled. I wrapped my arms around her and patted my hands all over her shirt, feeling for blood. I was sixteen. All I could think was that she had been jumped or robbed on her way in the door. My boyfriend stood wide-eyed, frozen at the top of the stairs. I waved my arm, shooing him away from us. My mother sat up and pressed her forehead to the cold wall beside the bottom step. And then she told me everything.

I know there were plenty of stories I shouldn't have heard. Plenty of details I should never have known. I was so young. Maybe she should have protected me more. But if she couldn't tell me all of those things, who would have protected her?

My father packed his things and left the next day while I was at school. He sent me one text message the following day that read, "I know you're upset . . ." A half-sentence meant to illicit a response, I'm sure, but I could think of nothing to say.

Almost instinctually, I buried the devastated little girl who had just lost her family for the second time. That felt far too vulnerable, far too painful to go through again. I had to lock her away.

Instead, I reacted like any other teenager preoccupied with football games and siphoning vodka from the liquor cabinets of their friends' perfect parents. The only thing that angered me more than knowing my father had cheated was knowing that everyone else would know my father had cheated. I imagined my schoolmates' mothers, adorned in their pleated tennis skirts, smiling pitifully at me from the driver's seats of their SUVs. That poor curly-headed kid from the broken home.

I never answered the text message my father sent that day, or any that came in the following weeks. Then one day, they stopped coming altogether.

My father married the woman from the church choir in a wedding I was not invited to. Six years went by and the phone never rang. Some years, he would send a happy birthday text. Sometimes on the right day, but more often, on the wrong one.

On my eighteenth birthday, a bouquet of white roses was left on the doorstep with a card that played "Somewhere Over the Rainbow" when I opened it. I threw it all in the garbage, recalling that Valentine's night when there had been no roses for me. When my father had given them all to someone else.

It would be unfair to say he didn't try a few times over the years. In my stubbornness, I just wanted him to try harder. I wanted him to show up to my swim meets whether I asked him to or not. I wanted to peer up into the bleachers through fogged-up goggles and see his tall, unmistakable frame among all the other parents. I wanted to roll my eyes that he was there, but feel my heart flutter that he had come. I wanted him to fight for me. I wanted him to call me Goose. He'd called me that my whole life. Why did I have to go looking for him first? I was the kid. He was the dad.

I cried to my mom about it all the time in the beginning. I wanted to know what happened. I wanted to know how someone goes months . . . years without knowing a single thing about their own child.

One evening, on the car ride home from swim practice, my mother spoke extensively about how excited my dad had been when we were born. "Everything was so fun when you and James were toddlers," she said, smiling. "Your dad was just over the moon." I asked how one goes from being over the moon to being out of the picture.

"Teenagers are tough, Brianna," she said. "You're a tough cookie. After a while, I think your dad didn't know how to handle the hard stuff. I think he was scared of you."

My breath caught in my throat. I looked over at her, dumbfounded, but she stared straight ahead over the wheel. My father was scared of me. What kind of kid's own father is scared of them? Better yet, was that his fault or mine? It was information I never quite knew what to do with. Still don't.

So I leaned into it. I decided I would be as tough and as stubborn a kid as he'd ever seen. I graduated high school, went to college, fell in love with Neil . . . all without a word to or from my dad.

In my senior year of high school, a friend's father died suddenly of heart failure. I sat at the funeral and sobbed. I sobbed for her loss, of course, but I also sobbed for the deeply shameful pang of envy I felt for a brief moment. At least with death, you can mourn. It feels much hollower when someone simply disappears.

Perhaps it was the loss of so much that made me want so little. The less I had, the less I'd have to inevitably part with. When I lay there inside that old rusted van on those exquisitely manicured Salt Lake City streets, it felt as though I knew something all those people didn't.

Perhaps it sounds strange, but those perfectly ordinary people with their perfectly ordinary lives seemed, to me, like the crazy ones. Didn't they know how precarious their happiness was? Didn't they know how quickly all those delicate and beautiful things could disappear?

In the silence of those nights, it occurred to me that the desire to create a life kept entirely within arm's reach was seeded somewhere deeply in the losses of my childhood. And yet I lay there, smug in the idea that I had found a loophole to inevitable tragedy; convinced I could avoid any more of the pain I'd already survived.

Grief comes to us in many forms. In those moments, mine had simply disguised itself as wisdom.

For most van-dwellers and transients, going down to Baja or Central America each December was practically an expected pilgrimage. "Why don't you just drive to Mexico?" people would say, as if it were as simple as going to the grocery store. The truth was, we did drive to Mexico, albeit not for a whole season.

One afternoon in a fit over my small propane heater breaking for the third time, I decided that Mexico was just the ticket. The only problem was that I had to be at my job until at least 3:00 p.m. on Fridays and Neil had to be back at his job by 6:00 a.m. on Wednesdays. That gave us a little over ninety-six hours to get to Mexico and back.

We mapped a course that would take us south through Nevada, weaving into California, and eventually arriving at the Mexicali border crossing, where we would bear east and head for the Sea of

Cortez. It was the picture-perfect image of the American Southwest. Nothingness for miles, coyotes crossing cactus-framed roads, and a couple of long-haired kids bound for the Mexican border in an old orange bus.

At the border crossing, we gathered our passports and the necessary vaccine paperwork for the dogs. Men and women approached the waiting line of cars trying to sell their cowboy hats and bottled water. A lanky, shirtless gentleman took a running leap up onto Bertha's thirty-three-inch front tire and began cleaning our windshield, refusing to take no for an answer. Heat rose off the pavement as hundreds of cars idled in wait. Border Patrol officials being half-dragged by drug-sniffing dogs weaved between each vehicle and lingered near our back bumper as Bucket and Dagwood whined through the window. A young man in a VW bus threw us a wave from a couple of lanes over.

It is pertinent to mention that Neil spoke not a single word of Spanish and I hadn't utilized the language since the last day of eighth grade, when my class performed a song called "Quiero el Beefsteak." So outside of singing about meat or asking a teacher where the bathroom was, we were relying entirely on a small list of phrases we had translated and written down, including, but not limited to: Can we camp here? How much does this cost? Have you seen my dog?

None of these phrases came in handy as Bertha rolled into the customs stall and promptly died right there, with her front tires in Mexico and her back tires in the United States.

Three female Border Patrol officers approached our windows, yelling things in Spanish as Neil and I stared in disbelief at each other. We popped the front hood, and peered, on tiptoes, into the steaming engine compartment. This gesture tends to be universal for *We're fucked* no matter what language you speak.

"I think it's just overheated," Neil said in a desperate attempt to convince himself.

The crowd of uniformed, armed, and annoyed Border Patrol officers continued to grow beside the van as other cars were waved into adjacent lanes. I turned around to face them and yelled, "It's just overheated . . . it's . . . it's just hot. *Caliente! Caliente!*"

It wasn't until later that I was able to fully appreciate the image of a barefoot American girl in velvet bell-bottoms standing in front of a gigantic van, flapping her arms and screaming, "*Caliente! Caliente!*"

When the second-grade Spanish vocabulary failed me, I attempted to distract the officials by offering up our passports and paperwork while Neil smacked various hoses and valves under the hood with a hammer. One woman snatched our passports from my hand and shouted, "How long?!"

"Three days," I smiled, holding my fingers up like a toddler.

In the chaos, she must have thought I said three months or three years or God knows what, because she immediately pointed over to a building and shouted, "Visa!"

"No . . . no visa! I looked it up, no visa," I pleaded. She shoved the passports back into my hands, leaned in toward me, and growled, "Visa," before storming off.

By now, it had been a full twenty minutes that Bertha had been sitting directly on the international border. Bucket and Dagwood had accepted that this was not the beach they had been promised and went back to sleep on the bed.

Every few minutes, a different officer would walk over to the window, stare at us, shake their head, and then walk back over to the group to likely report that the hippies were still broken down over there.

With each new face that appeared at our window, we cranked on Bertha's starter, rubbing her dashboard like an old dog's head, shouting words of encouragement. Finally, on our sixth or seventh attempt, Bertha sprung to life with a violent shudder and Neil floored the gas pedal to keep her from falling back to sleep.

I leaned my whole upper body out the window and yelled over to my officer friend, "Visa?!" She, along with three or four other officers, began waving us forward, shouting furiously, "Go! Jus' go!" And off we went into Mexico.

We followed directions onto Carretera San Felipe–Mexicali and out of the bounds of the city. The farther we drove, the more frightening the idea of breaking down again became. Our cell phones didn't work in this country, we didn't speak the language, and we had everything we valued in our life on board.

After about two hours of burnt brown desert hills, I squinted over the steering wheel at what appeared to be a tollbooth off in the distance. We were relieved to see signs of life, even if we couldn't communicate with them.

The long-awaited tollbooth turned out to be a military checkpoint. Five or six men in full khaki-colored uniforms approached the van and ordered us to get out. I was, once again, barefoot on the hot pavement.

For a full thirty minutes, those men tore Bertha apart as she sat idling in the middle of the highway. We were far too nervous to shut her off for fear that she might never turn on again. They lifted up our mattress, tore off our sheets, opened drawers, and overturned boxes while we sat on the curb with the dogs beneath a giant sign (in English!) that read, MONITOR YOUR BELONGINGS DURING SEARCH.

One overly friendly officer was curious about the black PVC pipe mounted to the top of the van that we had been using as a makeshift shower. I could think of nothing other than to mime the action of taking a shower beneath it until his eyes lit up and he gave a big thumbs-up.

Once they had searched just about every inch of the van, they signaled for us to get back inside. Before we drove away, one soldier climbed back in through the sliding door and asked me to open my purse. Then he asked me to open my wallet. Then my sunglass case. The tip of his automatic rifle pressed into Bertha's fabric ceiling as he leaned over my shoulder. Without moving an inch, he lifted his eyes to meet mine and, with a big mustached grin, whispered, "*Where's the marijuana?*"

Perhaps they sensed how nervous the two of us were, which had nothing to do with smuggling drugs into Mexico, and everything to do with our half-broken van. But really, I think those good ol' boys were just disappointed to come up empty-handed after two kids blasting Creedence Clearwater from a Scooby Doo van came barreling toward them out of the desert dust.

I still had a white-knuckle grip on the wheel as I watched the military checkpoint disappear in the rearview mirror while the Sea of Cortez came into view in turquoise off to the left. Downtown San Felipe had an eerie feel to it, as though we had arrived either a little too early or a little too late. For what, I wasn't sure.

A couple of local kids cruised past us on mopeds while an older American-looking couple pulled out of a gas station in a dune buggy and threw us a wave. We pulled down the very first dirt two track that looked like it headed toward the beach.

At the end of the road was a man with dreadlocks so long, they drew a little semicircle in the sand when he turned toward the sound of our engine. Neil jumped out with a piece of paper in his hand and ran over. Through my rolled-down window, I heard his forced attempt at Spanish as he asked if we could camp here. The man cracked a broad, yellow-toothed smile and pointed a firm finger toward the ground, exclaiming, "Yes! Here!" After Neil handed him twenty bucks, we pulled a couple hundred yards farther down the beach, slid the door open, and collapsed in the sand.

In spite of all the van troubles and the language barriers and the marijuana shakedowns, in spite of the fact that we had just forty-eight hours until we had to turn around and drive right back, that will always be one of my favorite misadventures.

By the time we rolled back into Utah, we would have driven 1,700 miles just to dip our toes in a body of water we'd not touched before. Thirty-four hours round-trip just to peer out a passing window at a part of the world we'd not yet seen; to lie in the sun and watch our dogs swim out into the sea, chasing all those tricky diving ducks.

And I don't believe it ever really occurred to me just how crazy that was.

I could feel myself starting to shift. My coworkers always loved to gather round my desk and hear what I'd been up to, but it was the stories of near-disaster that kept them transfixed. "What did you do then?" they would ask, wide-eyed, over my computer screen.

I began reveling in their reactions, overly eager to share all the gory details. I recalled, with great enthusiasm, nights of snake oil tow truck drivers; nights of having to pee into a Pringles can because I'd lost my plastic funnel.

Disgust crept across their faces, as if a child had just stuck out a tongue full of chewed food. But their reactions emboldened me. Their disapproval somehow made me feel I was on the right track. All we truly end up being in this life are the stories we can tell. I intended to make them good ones.

Our best friends lived on the corner of a busy street. There was public parking on either side, but only for certain hours. This would mean that I could sleep on one side beginning at 8:00 p.m., but I needed to wake up and perform a three-point turn to park on the other side before 7:00 a.m.

It was a bizarre ritual, jutting out into rush-hour morning traffic for forty-five seconds and then climbing back into bed. Some mornings I could hardly remember if I'd even gotten up to do it. I'd peel back the silver Reflectix insulation to check which side of the road I was on. I suppose muscle memory kicks in when you're fixed in that half-place between asleep and awake.

One night on the northbound shoulder, I was jostled awake by the van shaking. I thought, perhaps, it was a garbage truck blowing past, but it was still pitch-black out. Suddenly there was creaking on the roof rack. I shot up from my pillow, wide awake now with the adrenaline surge that comes from the realization that someone is climbing on your van.

Bucket and Dagwood burst into a frenzy of howling so loud that the man on top fell the full eight feet to the ground, landing flat on his back before hobbling off in visible pain.

It wasn't the first time someone had attempted to break into the van while I slept alone inside of it. On a previous summer morning, I was on the street next to a church parking lot when the van started that telltale shaking. I could hear grunting on the other side of the thin metal frame, mere inches from my head.

A man had noticed that my mountain bike was locked to the bike rack, but the bike rack was not locked to the van. In clear morning light, he had backed his white van up to mine and begun heaving and pulling at the entire rack.

Shocked at his audacity, here on this quiet suburban street, I cracked the back window open and screamed, "Are you fucking serious?!"

That man must have jumped four feet off the ground. In terror, he stumbled backward and leapt into the driver's seat without even shutting his back doors. He drove off but, to my amazement, stopped only a few dozen feet down the road and got out to close them.

Without a second thought, I jumped from the bed, rocketed the sliding door open, and sprinted down the street after him in hopes of catching a license plate number.

I was barefoot, sporting nothing but underwear and a Stevie Nicks T-shirt. Bucket and Dagwood had, of course, followed me out the door and were now joyfully sprinting down the center of the road without collars and without a clue what we were chasing.

The white van disappeared around the corner as I slowed to a stop, bending over my knees to catch my breath. The dogs wriggled with anticipation, panting, curious if we might all chase the next car that came by too. A woman—her jaw agape in horror—watched from her driveway as I walked back down the street toward Bertha, barefoot and half-naked, Dagwood peeing on each passing tree.

I would be lying if I claimed those incidents didn't spook me, but they also provided some much-needed clarity. I grew up—as most women do—believing that the world was inherently dangerous. These narratives were most often pushed by people who had never truly gone out to see for themselves. Why would they? They had been traumatized by the nightly news and the horror movies and the wide-eyed stories whispered from one woman to another.

It's a profitable business, the business of fear. For every terrifying scenario, there is a strategically placed antidote for sale alongside it. I spent many nights alone in the van beneath streetlights or blackened desert skies wishing that I could snap my fingers and erase all the stories I'd been told, but I couldn't.

If I was going to do these things alone, I was going to have to do them afraid. I would not let societally induced fear be a placeholder for the kind of life I wanted to live, and I swore to whisper this to myself every night until I actually believed it. There are many nights, even now, that I whisper it still.

The men who prowled the streets and found themselves heaving and tugging at my van didn't wish me any harm, per se. They just wanted to steal my shit. Perhaps they needed the money or perhaps it was some kind of cheap thrill. Whatever the reason, it was hardly as nefarious as I was anticipating.

One thing was certain: whether good or bad, Bertha drew attention everywhere. People constantly came up at gas stations or in parking lots asking what year she was, how many miles were on her, asking to take a look inside. Intersections and stoplights were almost always met with iPhone cameras poised in my direction. A mechanic once referred to the van as "Goldilocks's Bulldozer" when announcing over the loudspeaker that she was ready.

Children delighted at the sight of what appeared to be a real-life Tonka truck, and old hippies smiled and affectionately patted Bertha's hood, recounting the transient days from their own youths.

At a stoplight in Idaho, a gray-haired man caught sight of our *Hayduke Lives* bumper sticker—an ode to the late Edward Abbey—and shouted over through his open window, "Oh man, where's Ed when we need him, huh?"

As the light turned green, he held up a peace sign with fingers crinkled like papier-mâché and hollered, "Stay in trouble but stay out of jail. The soup's terrible!"

Bertha was brilliant at bringing all kinds of characters into my world.

Oftentimes, I couldn't even help but laugh walking toward her with arms full of grocery bags.

Amid a sea of family minivans and sensible sedans, Bertha loomed a solid five feet above them all like a parade float. I'd have sooner forgotten my own name before I forgot where I parked my car. She was impossibly large and impossibly orange and the concept that a woman was behind the wheel seemed, to some, the most impossible feature of all.

We were an odd couple, that van and me. Neil still had the pickup truck he used for work, but Bertha was my home *and* my car. It took only a few months for my driving skills to surpass Neil's entirely, sheerly for the fact that I had to parallel park that beast all over Salt Lake City. I learned every angle, studied every measurement. I could tell you from a quarter-mile away if she was going to fit into a parking space or not. I knew the speed she hummed the best at and the smoky-sweet smell of her coolant. I had heard every smart-ass sexist comment about where *a pretty little thing like me* learned to drive *a big old thing like that.*

Under the watchful eyes of long-haul truckers and gaunt-faced farmers, I teetered up the ladder to the roof rack with full five-gallon gas cans and bundles of firewood.

Since Neil was already down in the desert for work, I was always the one tasked with preparing the van for our trips to parts unknown. Stocking the cooler and topping off propane tanks and double-checking the container of assorted backup fluids that Bertha could begin leaking at any moment. Green was antifreeze; pink was transmission; reddish-black was engine oil. Things I now knew that I never imagined I would know.

With the van all lubed up and packed, I would meet Neil at some dirt road intersection or in the dusty parking lot of his field office and he'd hop up into the driver's seat. I was a bit like a sous-chef, prepping and organizing behind the scenes until the head chef burst through the kitchen's double doors carrying the meal and all the glory.

So I began planning trips out to the desert on my own. I wanted to feel as comfortable behind the wheel on dirt as I did on pavement. The truth of the matter was, I relied on Neil for almost everything. Knots in our climbing ropes. Coordinates to slot canyons. Correct answers in the roadside game of *What's That Burning Smell?*

Passersby on the highway and strangers on the internet alike had this idea of me that I wasn't even certain *I* believed. Sure, I drove a gnarly off-road vehicle and slept in it alone sometimes, and sure, I loved being covered in mud in deep cracks of the desert, but the fact that I'd hardly ever tackled an excursion on my own felt disingenuous. I was beginning to feel like I had yet another thing to prove.

Now, if you had sat across the cafeteria table from sixteen-year-old me and told me that I would one day be topping off fluids and checking the PSI on my tires and ensuring I had a shovel so I could dig holes to shit in, you would have been met with absolute horror, and understandably so.

The women I looked up to growing up were glamorous and beautiful and well dressed. They certainly weren't connoisseurs of camping, and I cannot imagine a single one of them had ever shit in a hole.

This was such a departure from who I thought I would be. I'd never seen anyone do this. So, was I doing this right? How would anyone tell me if I was doing this right? And how would I even know *how* to do something right if I didn't really know what I was doing at all?

As I turned off the pavement and onto the dirt road for my first solo trip, it occurred to me that I might have to be my own inspiration.

There is a stretch of desert in southern Utah that is even more nothing-y than most. A network of unnamed dirt roads carved aimlessly into fields dotted with cactus and sagebrush, popping up through pores of red dirt.

A long, lonesome drive west on Highway 70 winds past painted clay hills and distant buttes, past the San Rafael Swell reef—an upthrust of Wingate and Navajo sandstone that juts from the ground like the fins of a dinosaur's back. Like a mountain range made entirely of sandstone, complete with foothills of purple and turquoise-striped clay. It is, perhaps, the only feature around here that serves to remind passersby that this place once loomed deep beneath an ancient sea.

Twice in relatively recent history, this unassuming stretch of sand has found its way into the limelight. Butch Cassidy and the Sundance Kid—and many other members of their Wild Bunch gang—would hide out here between their famed horseback train heists and daring bank jobs in the late 1800s, ultimately giving this place the name it still bears today: Robbers Roost.

Though the West has long been won, the Roost is still about as wild as it comes these days. Two hundred sixty-five square miles of cell-service-less, four-wheel-drive, high-clearance roads that end mostly in old mines and towering cliff edges. The only reason you might find yourself out there today is for the technical canyoneering opportunities . . . or if your granddaddy's granddaddy had an open-range cattle permit and you've taken over the family business.

Beyond the big black bovines lie slot canyons hidden deep within the folds of the earth. Accessible only by rope and determination, and sometimes impassable from flash floods and obstacles. That's the kind of adventure a fellow named Aron Ralston was after back in 2003—the next time Robbers Roost made the headlines.

By a series of events he can tell you about in his *own* book, Ralston found himself stuck in a narrow slot canyon for five days without food and water, lodged in place by a boulder that had fallen and crushed his arm. With no options remaining, Ralston managed to extricate a dull two-inch pocketknife from his backpack and cut his own arm off.

You see, what Butch Cassidy and Aron Ralston both knew was that, out here, nobody's coming to find you.

I fell in love with the Roost for the reasons both of those famed men did—it was, and still is, a hideout of sorts. A place you go when you don't want to be found.

The Roost initially presents itself—like much of the desert—as nothing at all. With mountains, the beauty is right in front of you. Their grandeur can be seen from miles away. The shorelines and the coastal cliffs can be felt before you even arrive; telltale signs of cooler winds and sticky salt air, the call of gulls. But the desert is a bit trickier.

Cow-pie- and cactus-covered stretches of sand, dotted with the occasional juniper. Jackrabbits and beady-eyed lizards and that Western-movie whistle of wind and buzz of unforgiving heat. Some may find a place like that unnerving, even boring. They might drive a few miles down the road, maybe peer off a ledge into more vastness, and then turn to leave. They've seen all there is to see, they assume.

But then there are those who go farther, who tumble down miles and miles of dirt roads until those roads devolve into rocky two-track trails that wind and sink down between the buttresses. And when those tracks end, they forge their own on foot, winding through dried-up washes and aimless cattle trails carved through fields of half-bloomed rabbitbrush and Mormon tea. The sky narrows; the sandstone rises. In a world of instant gratification, the desert still calls to the determined.

In that spirit of determination, I chose Robbers Roost as the destination for my first solo trip. I rumbled along the lonesome sun-bleached highway until the time came to hook a hard left onto the dirt. Bertha's tires clattered loudly over a cattle grate as Bucket and Dagwood leapt back and forth between seats.

I jumped out to lock the manual hubs on Bertha's front tires. This was a very important thing to do, and I knew that because Neil had told me eighteen times before I left him in the parking lot of his office.

The road quickly devolved from small pebbles and gradual dips to deep ruts, jagged rocks, and washboard bumps that made it feel as though the van might vibrate right off her own axles.

I learned pretty quickly to stay off Bertha's brakes as I strained to see each obstacle through the dust- and dog-nose-smeared windshield. I'd catch sight of a rut in the road too late, or a little sand dune that had blown out across the red clay, and I'd simply let my foot off the gas and ride it out. Slamming on the brakes only made her hit harder, as if she tensed up in anticipation like her passengers. If I rolled straight through, it was rough, but it felt intentional and that, to me, was a fundamental difference when driving alone on dirt roads.

It didn't take long before I began to knowingly shift my hips with the rocking of her axles, like a cowboy learning to move with his horse. We were one entity rolling together.

I had left my office on a Friday afternoon, planning to be out there for four days. My mother was not pleased that I had chosen a place without cell service, but if I was going to learn to be on my own, I would have to sever *all* of my most precious lifelines.

As I drove farther and farther away from civilization, the sun began to sink. It seemed to hover just above the horizon for longer than usual, making reds more crimson and oranges more red. Kangaroo mice darted across the road, along with the occasional cottontail. Dusk in the desert was always the liveliest.

In the side-view mirror, I looked back at tall clouds billowing up like steam in deeply bruised tints of purple and blue. My heart rate quickened as far-off bolts of lightning hit the ground, their jagged silhouettes tearing through the darkness, as if the sky had been grabbed from either side and ripped apart.

Hot air steamed off of Bertha's hood as she bore forward and deeper into the dark. The forecast hadn't called for anything ominous, but the weather out here could scarcely be predicted anyway.

Storms like that were the authors of the desert. Building over the distant mountains, they'd swoop in and swallow the sky, rewriting the course of canyons and the direction of rivers. Torrents of rain uprooted junipers and overturned boulders. Winds pushed mammoth mountains of sand out over the roads, effortlessly erasing what men had toiled over.

Millions and millions of years' worth of those storms are the reason for the slot canyons that weave through the Roost like veins. Floodwater gathers in creeks and basins and rushes down over porous rock, eventually forming a canyon significantly deeper than it is wide. The Colorado Plateau in the US Southwest has the highest concentration of slot canyons in the world due to the marrying of these storms and sandstone. Some were a couple of feet wide and some just a few inches. Some were narrow and featureless and others looked like grand hallways made with sweeping strokes of a paintbrush.

No matter their appearance, to find yourself standing inside of one was to bear witness to a lucky combination of wind, water, and time. What would be rather unlucky, however, would be finding yourself in one of those canyons in a storm like the one brewing behind me.

Several times a season, news would come in that a group of tourists had died in a flash flood or that the water-warped remains of an experienced canyoneer were found in the aftermath of some severe weather. Most would assume that the cause of a death like that would be drowning, that the slot canyon would slowly begin to fill with water like some scene from an Indiana Jones movie. But the reality was much more violent.

Rainwater funneling through miles of ever-deepening canyons would pick up speed, and as it picked up speed, it would pick up anything in its path. Boulders as wide as your wingspan. Logs as thick as your torso. Cow carcasses and juniper roots and jagged rocks. You'd hear a low rumble first, then a deafening roar. Then a wall of desert debris would round a corner and crush you where you stood.

The desert is such a volatile place that I have often wondered what it is that I find so peaceful about it. Perhaps it's the silence. Perhaps it's the ancientness. Or perhaps it's the sheer intention of anything bold enough to grow there, to thrive there. I wanted to be in the desert, yes, but perhaps more important, I wanted to be *like* the desert.

At an unmarked intersection beneath Bertha's muted yellow ceiling light, I studied the screenshots I had taken of a topographical map. It was about twenty-one miles to the overlook I planned to camp on. Twenty-one miles, out here of course, could mean another two hours.

After firing Bertha's engine back up, I was surprised, but comforted to see a pair of headlights coming toward me. A dark green Subaru slowed to a stop and rolled the window down amid Bucket's and Dagwood's barking.

"You headed down that way?" a bearded man shouted up at me,

one passenger in the front seat and another in the back practically stuffed against the window beneath camping gear and backpacks.

"Yeah, I'm headed out toward the Angel's Point area," I replied, trying to sound like I knew where I was headed.

"Well, the sand dunes up there a little ways have totally taken the road out," he explained. "We spent a good hour or two trying to dig our way through, but it's just not happenin'." He glanced at my tires and smiled. "You let some air out of those things and you might actually be able to make it." I was thrilled by this total stranger's confidence in me.

By the time I reached the dunes, I could see clear evidence of the Subaru's struggle. Faint tire tracks, frantic claw marks, and an eventual defeated three-point turn marked the end of their attempt. I jumped down from the front seat as the dogs tumbled out the open door and disappeared into the darkness.

Standing there in the dim glow of Bertha's headlights, I examined the great pile of sand before me. It was eerie, but not uncommon. The Bureau of Land Management had been keeping a bulldozer in the area to clear the road for cattle ranchers, but they were less concerned with access for the thrill-seeking outdoorsmen. That Friday night, the road sat buried.

I climbed up onto the sand, my bare feet disappearing into the cool, shifting earth. Bucket's howling interrupted the silence as she and Dagwood darted out over the dunes, chasing a jackrabbit the size of a house cat. She was a terrible hunter, loudly announcing her presence, unable to contain her excitement. Dagwood followed on the side, silent, weaving effortlessly through junipers. If a rabbit was caught, it was almost always Dagwood who caught it.

The half-moon overhead provided just enough light for me to see where the dune receded and the road returned about two hundred feet ahead.

"I think we can make it," I whispered to Bucket, who had returned to my side, panting and pleased with herself. I climbed back in, started Bertha's engine, and shifted her into four-wheel-drive low. With a loud clank, she lurched forward, moving like molasses through the first few feet. When it got deeper, her tires spun in place, sending torrents of sand flying up on either side of my open windows. I jerked the wheel to the left and then to the right and then to the left again, trying to climb her up out of the holes she was digging herself. Frustrated, I reversed out of the sand and sat silent for a moment.

"I think we gotta floor it," I said aloud to the dogs, who reciprocated with silence, as they always did.

On the second attempt, I rolled a few car lengths back from the start of the dune and picked up a bit of speed. She glided through her previously torn track before bouncing violently up over the edge of it into freshly uncharted sand. I kept the pedal pressed, and her wheels spun accordingly, but the distance she traveled was mere inches at a time.

I was now about halfway through the dune, my knuckles ghost-white, gripping the wheel. Every inch forward meant one less inch downward. Even the briefest pause and she'd have sunk.

I reached the crest of the dune and let off the gas entirely, allowing the weight of the van to carry her down on the other side. For all the creaks and groans she usually made, Bertha fell totally silent for a moment, as if she were floating. A few more revs of the engine and the tires were back on dirt. I leapt from the van, whooping and hollering into the night sky as Bucket and Dagwood returned to their darkened wanderings.

I gazed, glowing, at my mangled tracks through the dune. They seemed to be disappearing by the second, as though the sand was swallowing any evidence of my victory.

I arrived at the overlook about an hour later, pulling into a clearing stomped out by cows. The engine was still searing hot from lumbering in four-wheel drive for hours and the air outside wasn't much better, even at almost midnight.

Overjoyed with my own bravery, I let out one final whoop before opening all the doors and falling asleep on top of the blankets beneath the frantic wings of feasting mosquitos and big silvery moths.

I was up by 6:00 a.m. the next morning, because to stay in bed past that point was akin to roasting oneself in a large oven. I pulled my box of kitchen supplies from the back and set up the small folding table and Coleman camp stove. Bucket stood diligently over the remnants of an old firepit, tail wagging methodically. She had been after the same lizard for almost an hour now.

I spent a good long while trying to attach the propane tank to the stove but each time I pressed it to the valve, it seemed to spray compressed gas out of the top, burning my nostrils. I paced back and forth a few times, wondering how likely it was that this small tank would explode the moment I touched a lighter to the stove.

It was sobering to realize how many things Neil did without my even realizing he did them. Here I thought I was some pioneer woman, yet I couldn't even light a stove. Unable to call anyone or google anything, I simply accepted that I might be blown to smithereens and screwed the tank down until the frigid propane pouring out of either side went silent. I held my breath as the lighter touched the burner and watched, elated, when the flames jumped to life. Another victory.

While water for my coffee boiled, I went about unzipping and unrolling the awning over the sliding door. Staking one side down, I'd run to the other side and try to stand that one up before the other side fell back down again. I must have smacked my head on the metal poles a dozen times.

With breakfast made and a square of shade provided, I sat in a camp chair and stared out at it all. When the coffee in my cup started to get low, I considered making another. My skin tingled with mosquito bites and scabs from the gnats and no-see-ums.

Truthfully, I was a bit lost out there. No one to talk to, no schedule to stick to. I could have sat in that chair for three straight days and not one single person in the world would care. I was surprised by how unnerving it was. I was surprised at how hard it was to just . . . be.

Out beyond my campsite, otherworldly pale pink domes stretched for as far as the eye could see. Petrified sand dunes, they were called. Hundreds of thousands of years of sand solidifying into rock, preserving the visible layers that built them up in the first place. If these were petrified dunes, I liked to think of slot canyons as petrified wind. Both representations of time, frozen in time themselves.

I stood up to start packing my backpack, carefully pouring water from my five-gallon blue jug into three separate bottles. One for me and one for each dog. A fourth bottle was filled with the wine I had planned to drink the night before but had been far too exhausted. I packed a camera and sunscreen and a short rope with a carabiner attached, which Neil said could be useful if I needed to lower the dogs down or haul the dogs up.

Surveying the canyons from the edge of the bluff, I mapped the easiest route. The plan was to wind our way down to the Dirty Devil—a river so muddy, I could scarcely see my own foot in four inches of it.

We descended down the slope of the first petrified dune, Bucket's and Dagwood's nails scratching chalky white trails on the sandstone. With each layer we dropped, strange rock formations rose up around us like Dr. Seuss trees.

The fact that the landscape in the desert always seemed to be crumbling provided a kind of urgency, a kind of frantic possessiveness to the way I thought about this place. I had to see it all before it was no longer there to be seen. I had to mentally document it in as many of its forms as possible, lest I never got the chance to again. Lest it crumble before my very eyes.

The dogs reached the river before I did. I knew because the swooshing of the tall grasses they were running through gave way to splashing. Bucket ran back to greet me before I'd even made it down, her brindled coat perfectly half-soaked and dripping.

The water was a foot deep at its deepest and nonexistent at its shallowest. Sawdust-colored rings around the base of the trees meant there were beavers afoot, and the dogs diligently began their patrol. Deeper pools had formed in certain places along the riversides where carp and catfish were stuck and flapping violently against the frantic pecking of birds. They spread their wings territorially every time Bucket or Dagwood came too close.

I dropped my backpack on a little sandbar, opened the water bottle of wine, and began wandering my way down the center of the river. The water level was so low, it's a wonder they even called it a river. And yet by desert standards, this place was buzzing with life. Vibrant green cottonwood trees lined either side of the water, providing shade for the free-range cattle who could be seen chewing idly, their heads peeking over the tall grass. The river was framed by sheer red walls scarred by long stretches of black varnish.

There were very few ways in and very few ways out, which is why I'd left my backpack as a marker for where to exit when I returned. I was also fully planning on being a bit buzzed by then.

After a mile or so of walking, the dogs tore off after some rustle in the brush. I listened as their barking grew more and more distant. Whatever they were chasing, I knew they likely wouldn't catch it.

Digging my wine bottle into the sand, I stripped off my tank top and shorts and lay down on my back in six inches of water, naked as the day I came. With only my ears submerged, each muffled sound from the dogs, each tinkling of sand floating past my head sounded unfamiliar, but comforting. Like sounds we hear from the womb.

My hair swayed in slow motion like seaweed.

Each day thereafter, we made our way back down to the river. I hadn't seen another person since the dark-green Subaru. Statistically speaking, the closest people to me were the folks flying overhead in commercial airplanes. I squinted up at one. I wondered where they were going.

That day, I wasn't at all afraid to be in what is, arguably, the most vulnerable state. Naked and alone. Everything about the remoteness of this place and all its hidden corners made me feel surprisingly safe. Far safer than anywhere in any city.

I never knew walls could be that big or rocks could be that red or silence could be that silent. I certainly never knew skies could be that blue. For four straight days, I was the only person in the world.

Bucket and Dagwood would disappear for long periods of time, exploring with their noses to the ground and a lightness to their steps. Dagwood liked to stand belly-deep in the water with his tail wagging methodically, waiting for a beaver to emerge from the hole it had disappeared down.

The summer before, he had been tiptoeing the shores of the Colorado River when he very suddenly plunged his head into the shallows and came up with a full-grown beaver in his mouth. He shook it like a rag doll as I ran toward him, screaming. Dagwood let out a yelp as the beaver sliced its teeth directly into his nose.

By the time I reached them, the beaver lay on its back, taking its last heaving breaths before falling still. With tears in my eyes, I plucked a few black-eyed Susans from the riverside and laid them on top of him as Dagwood stood over me, beaming. He'd had a taste for beavers ever since.

I'd often cut my trips short by a day or two in the early stages of my solo adventuring. I missed Neil. I wanted to run to him and tell him all the things I'd done, the cliffs I'd scaled, the dunes I'd conquered. The moment my phone dinged with signs of cell service, I'd dial his number. We would meet in the parking lot of his field office and run into each other's arms. He was proud of me. He looked at me as though I could do anything. When I showed photos to his parents or retold tales of my adventures to groups of friends across restaurant tables, he would watch me, beaming. His confidence in me was ultimately what pushed me further. My trips became longer, more daring, but I was still a creature of habit. I spent most of my time in a rotating series of three or four different expanses of desert. The upside to that was that the roads I traveled out there were ones I came to memorize. I knew each and every curve of the sandstone spires that cast all those golden-hour shadows. I knew which cattle gates rattled the loudest beneath the tires. My soul read the rocks in the road like braille on a page. Every time I took that familiar left turn onto the dirt and drove past the ROADS MAY BE IMPASSABLE sign, I felt a great sense of relief.

After all, Bertha had already proven herself extremely capable of passing. I imagine this is how all my friends back east must have felt pulling into their driveways.

The thought that I might be in danger when I was alone in the desert was not something that occurred to me very often, if at all. Living in a van in the middle of a city felt far more dangerous. People all smashed up against one another in parking lots and apartment buildings and crowded shopping malls, cussing each other out over the steering wheel, pounding broom handles against the ceilings like Morse code.

It's easy to take other human beings for granted in places like that. There're too many to count, too many to name. They're just another part of the landscape, another *thing*. It was those environments that made me untrustworthy of other people.

Out in the desert, it was just some cattle ranchers in their pickup trucks and a couple of enthusiastic outdoorsmen. Real remote dirt-road etiquette has two fundamental rules: One is to throw a wave and a wide girth as you pass other vehicles. The other is to pick a spot to camp that is not even remotely near another human being.

Nobody drives all the way the hell out there to look at someone else's Toyota Tacoma glistening on the horizon. They went out there to be alone too. And alone is exactly what I was one beautiful spring afternoon when I rounded a canyon corner and stumbled, headlong, into a wild-eyed man crouched in the shadow of a juniper tree beneath the beating midday sun.

I don't know who yelled louder upon the sight of each other, but the commotion brought the dogs careening around the corner, barking wildly. Bucket was incredibly sweet natured, but her bark could be terrifying. She looked positively rabid, spit flying from her jowls, as she growled and lunged from the safety of between my legs. Dagwood stood a few feet in front of me with his hackles raised like a hyena.

He was only a body's length away from the man, who now stood with his arms raised, palms facing me. The universal sign for "I mean no harm." But the dogs were not convinced.

That was the first time I felt it. Buzzing in my knees and rattling in my rib cage and radiating up my spine to the hairs on the back of my neck; the closest thing we humans have left to our *own* hackles. Fear.

I had only intended to go out for a few days to a fresh spring Neil and I had visited once before. He had taken the small roll of tin used to block out wind on our Jetboil backpacking stove and folded it into a funnel of sorts. We didn't even filter it, just drank it straight from the crack in the wall it trickled out of.

There weren't any "trails" out there besides the ones stomped out by the ambling of cows, so the river acted as the trail. Walking straight through sometimes-thigh-, sometimes-ankle-deep water for miles was exhausting, but it beat traversing over land in hundred-degree weather. It also meant I didn't have to pack extra water for the dogs.

I parked Bertha on a cliff's edge a few miles away and followed steep sandstone slopes downward toward the burst of green cottonwood trees that marked the sign of flowing water. My course was rarely direct. Many of the rocky slopes dropped off suddenly, but it was near impossible to tell until I was standing at the edge. Finding a safe way down meant spending hours searching for a spot that was gradual enough to scramble down, and reasonable enough to eventually scramble back up.

Fortunately, Bucket and Dagwood could cover three times as much ground as me and would drop each level with relative ease, mapping a path for me to follow. Sometimes I would approach the obstacles they jumped down with total disbelief. They had grown to be as strong and as agile as the big-horned sheep they loved to scout for. I was grateful for that as they both stood between me and the man in the desert.

He had what seemed to be a permanent scowl beneath the brim of his woven sun hat. The skin I could see was leathery brown. The rest was hidden under a course blondish-white beard. He was covered in dirt and his clothes were unkempt. But that was something he and I had in common.

Over the roar of Bucket's barking, he removed his hat and

crouched low to the sand, extending an arm out toward her. She grumbled, hesitantly leaning forward while Dagwood now ran straight over and started licking his face.

"I'm Carl," he said. "Man, you scared me."

His voice was soft, like a grandfather's.

We sat up against the shaded side of the wall. I pulled out a granola bar as he began to make small talk. He was easily in his sixties. A real Edward Abbey–lookin' fella.

The dogs lay beneath the long early-morning shadow of sagebrush while he regaled me with stories of what Moab was like in the nineties. There weren't any Hilton hotels . . . let's just say that.

Turns out, he'd been coming out here for about thirty years now, wandering the rims and bagging every slot canyon and down-climbing to the river where he could. "It's a place that hasn't changed much," he said, but he was disappointed to find that his usual route down to the river had been washed out since his last trip.

I told him I had a way down that I was certain was still intact. He was reluctant to follow me. I mean . . . there I was, sports bra, cowboy hat, and a couple of crazy dogs in tow. "I checked it out over here already," he said, gruffly.

I smirked. "Well . . . that's definitely the way down, so are you comin' or not?" He chuckled as he steadied himself on the cliff edge.

We followed the path of least resistance down as he audibly doubted each turn I was making. I assured him I knew where I was going, but we still bickered like an old married couple the whole way.

Finally, I pointed down to a pile of rockfall that was not nearly as steep as it appeared. He opened his mouth to protest before looking down to see Bucket and Dagwood sprinting straight to the water.

I went first, turning to give him a spot with my knee at the base. He was reluctant to take that too, and made sure to mention that his lower back hadn't been the same since his late fifties. I smiled, knowing how these rural folks operate. A woman? Showing *them* the way? And a young one at that?

It's awfully frowned upon now, but there was something sweet about an old, crusty local assuming I was some damsel in distress. One, because they're well-meaning, and two, because it makes it a lot more fun to prove them wrong.

Once we had finally reached the ground, we took one more water break, sitting together in a patch of dirt clay stomped down to near-concrete by cattle. Then, we shook hands and went our separate ways. He was off to photograph a remote pictograph panel, and I was off to laze about in the river.

As he turned to leave, he looked back over his shoulder, silver beard in the sun, and said, "Well, Bri . . . you're alright."

And I *was* alright. In fact, I was better than I'd ever been. I had begun to feel like I belonged out here; like perhaps, someday, some young explorer might stumble upon me, crouched wild-eyed and gray-haired between all those red rocks.

We were fireside when the clock struck midnight, marking the end of Christmas Eve and the very early beginning of Christmas Day. It was our very first Christmas in the van.

I had made a trip to our storage unit in Salt Lake to retrieve a box of decorations my mom had given me. Some of them were heirlooms, stockings and ornaments I remember hooking onto the branches of our Christmas trees, my dad hoisting me up by the waist.

The dogs had long since fallen asleep beneath burrows of blankets inside the van. In the stillness of desert air, the sky was practically silver with constellations and hazy far-off galaxies. The kind of light beyond the light I could only see once I'd left the bounds of the modern world. The crackling fire was the only thing that broke the silence until I started reading a little something aloud that I had written to Neil.

When I finished, I lifted my gaze to find him staring just beyond my shoulder, one trembling finger aimed into the darkness. No more than six feet behind me, framed in a clearing of junipers, a coyote stared right back.

His front legs were spread slightly, head bowed, triangular snout to the earth, but his gaze tracked upward right into mine. I could see the orange reflection of our fire in the gloss of his eyes. He probably wasn't expecting us to be there; after all, no one else was. We sat in total silence, the three of us, motionless, staring at one another.

After a good long while, I reached for my camera, but he melted backward into the velvet night before I had even touched my fingers to it. We sat there in a sacred kind of silence long after he had left.

It was in instances like this that I began to notice how much I was changing. I suppose I should have been afraid, and there were still times that I was. But fear is one of the few things that remains the same between animal and man.

I had seen it in the tilted heads of tiny lizards assessing the threat of my passing shadow. I had seen it in the moon-eyed owls that flew low overhead in the solitude of slot canyons, their beating wings as rhythmic as breath. I had seen it in the beady eyes of rattlesnakes, tucked into the cracks and crevices of great sandstone monoliths. And I saw it there, in the first moments of Christmas Day, in the eyes of a coyote who lingered in the fading light of our fire.

Fear and curiosity. Those, to me, became the essentials of being alive. Alive in a simple, profound kind of way. The kind of alive we slowly weeded out when we built our cities and fenced our yards.

• • •

Neil and I both began to feel at ease out there in such an extreme place. Things we would have once considered outlandish became positively normal.

We would climb on top of the van and pour a five-gallon jug of water into the PVC pipe we called our shower. It took us a few tries before we knew exactly what time of day the water was warm, but not too warm. Attempting a shower after Bertha had been sitting in the sun all afternoon would likely have resulted in second-degree burns.

We would lie in two inches of lukewarm stream water, attempting any relief from the three-digit temperatures. At night, we would soak T-shirts in our water jugs and lay them over the top of our chests. It made triple-digit breezes significantly more pleasant, though we did have to hang the sheets out to dry each morning. One afternoon, we purchased an inflatable plastic baby pool from a dollar store and lined the bottom with our sleeping pads. We parked Bertha near a small bridge and road our bikes farther up the dirt road that traced the river. Neil balanced the already-inflated baby pool on his head. He looked like a gigantic rainbow jellyfish rolling through the starkness of the desert. A mile or so up the road, we dropped our makeshift boat into the river and floated with the current right back down to Bertha. The dogs ran alongside us on the riverbanks, weaving in and out of the shallow waters, splashing us as we stared up at the sky. On Neil's thirtieth birthday, we made another stop at the dollar store for a huge inflatable rubber duck and strapped it to his climbing harness at the edge of a two-hundred-foot cliff. I rappelled down first, landing in the shallow waters of a canyon that fills with water only every few years. I cackled with laughter, watching him dropping down from the sky with a gigantic yellow pool toy hanging below him like cargo.

The desert was our playground. We were kids out there. Those little dirty-faced ones with an unmistakable perfume of sunscreen and bug spray. Discomfort became something that no longer fazed us. It was practically a part of the fun. We liked the struggle of keeping ourselves alive like any other wild thing out there that appears, for a fleeting moment, between the junipers.

There is one slot canyon in Utah whose guidebook description is far more daunting than others. It is one of the narrowest passable slot canyons in the world, averaging nine to ten inches wide at its smallest, and about twenty-four inches at its widest. Even at just a quarter-mile long, it takes expert canyoneers three to four hours to pass through. To fully appreciate this canyon's constrictions, it should be mentioned that there is a weight limit listed in the beta. Anyone over 180 pounds, any woman with a large cup size, or any man bearing a particularly built chest *will not pass through.*

Now, as is the nature of any human endeavor, there are folks who do not heed these warnings. They can be found many hours—or sometimes days—later being doused with buckets of dish soap and hoisted out like ship freight by search-and-rescue ropes. (That's a true story, by the way.)

Despite the fact that Neil and I were relatively new to canyoneering, we felt confident we could make the passage and spare the soap. There was, however, just one catch. We planned to navigate this ever-tapering crack in the earth with two dogs in tow. Two dogs that were under 180 pounds, of course.

This was by no means Bucket and Dagwood's first slot canyon. A year earlier, when a friend offered to take us canyoneering for the first time, we left the dogs to nap in his room as we crawled our way through our first technical canyon. All the while, I kept whispering to Neil, "The dogs could've gotten over this . . ." or "The dogs could've handled that . . ."

The very next day, emboldened solely by possibility, we began researching harnesses. Outside of the heavy-duty search-and-rescue K9 gear, there was one company called Ruffwear that made a strength-rated harness designed specifically for rappelling a dog. I cannot imagine it was one of their bestsellers.

Several days after the package arrived with their gray and red double-backing harnesses, we set out to run through a mellow set of canyons called Ding and Dang. Bucket and Dagwood navigated the obstacles with ease, leaping over boulders and crawling beneath lodged logs. There was only one moment of sheer panic when we attached the rope to their harnesses and lowered them for the first time. Bucket was convinced we were pushing her off a cliff, her legs stiffening out to the sides, belly sliding unwillingly across the ground. But as soon as she realized she was attached to something, she settled. Neil lowered her a little over fifteen feet into a shallow pool where I stood waiting with arms wide.

We celebrated with excessive treats and encouragement, then repeated the same with Dagwood.

Not being much for easing into things, we decided we were immediately ready for bigger rappels. So, the following day, we ran through a six-hour slot canyon with a series of drops ranging from eighteen to eighty feet. Neil would rig up a rope anchor using some natural feature like a boulder or a log lodged between the canyon walls, or my favorite technique: the Dead Man's Anchor. This involves wrapping a rope around a rock, then burying that rock, then slowly weighting it and praying you don't fall backward to your death.

For the dogs, we crafted two short ropes as permanent tandem rappelling mechanisms that would allow us to secure them from two points: their harness to the rope, and their harness to our harness. Ultimately, they would end up perched on top of our laps, giving us the ability to maneuver backward down big drops with more agility than if they were just hanging beneath our bodies like cargo.

For however unusual a hobby it was, the dogs became tremendously skilled at it almost immediately. Bucket learned to perch across the top of my thighs as I stemmed over deep sections of canyon with my back pressed to one side and my feet to the other. Dagwood could leap over five-foot boulders without so much as a walking start.

By the time we were packing up for one of the narrowest canyons known to man, they had completed over twenty-five different slot canyons and dozens of drops ranging from 15 to 220 feet. Despite all this, we were still far more confident than we deserved to be.

We set out with our smallest possible packs, one short rope for the dogs, a couple of snacks, and about a gallon of water each. Most slot canyons hold some sort of standing water, which the dogs would usually lap up. Sometimes it was ankle deep; other times we were swimming through it. Despite the stagnant, slimy nature of that water, the dogs never once got sick, a fact we simply chalked up to years of exposure.

We scaled over the top of more petrified sand dunes, before down-climbing into a narrow wash that would ultimately lead us to the mouth of the slot canyon. With very little warning, the sanded path we followed plunged suddenly downward like a waterless waterfall between narrow red rock. We stood there staring like kids frozen at the top of the slide. No way out but through. So, in we went.

Scraping sounds are inevitable when squeezing your way through such tight quarters, but within the first thirty feet, one of our backpacks had already torn. Through the hole in the blue fabric, the tightly coiled red rope looked like intestines that might spill out at any minute.

We slid and climbed and scooched downward until a large sandy pothole appeared at the bottom. Most slot canyons make perfect sense when you think about how water flows over rock. We had slid down the part where water entered this canyon, and we would land in the spot where it would pool once the storm had passed. It was only slightly muddy when my feet hit it, meaning it likely hadn't rained in a while.

At this point, I expected to turn and see the usual path through a slot canyon: narrow walls, winding sandy ground to follow, perhaps a few obstacles or a drop requiring a rope. Instead, I found myself standing in an almost perfectly circular room of rock, about ten feet in diameter.

I was still scanning it in a panic when Neil dropped down behind me, followed closely by the skidding of the dogs' paws against the sandstone. There was a distinct reason we never once had to clip their nails.

"Neil, this can't be right," I said. "It's a dead end."

I only took two steps farther into the dimly lit chamber before I saw that it wasn't a dead end after all. Like an optical illusion, a slight shift in my stance revealed a thin, angular crack in the wall. Neil stepped around me and peered in.

"I think . . . I think this is the way . . ." he said, bewildered but excited.

Before I could protest, Dagwood disappeared into the base of the crack with Bucket close on his heels. Ironically, of all canyons, this one seemed almost designed *for* them. Smaller, more frequent rainstorms and floodwaters had carved out a little subway-like tunnel at the bottom of the larger crack we were to sidestep through. They scurried through it like mice beneath the floorboards. The catch, of course, was that it was still too narrow for them to turn around. Once they went forward, they had to keep moving forward, which meant we had to keep moving forward too.

We swore at ourselves and vowed to keep them firmly between the two of us when we caught up to them, but first we had to heave ourselves into this diagonal crack. We removed the backpacks from our backs, realizing we would need to drag them behind us if we were to fit through, and shimmied our way up and in.

It was quite like lying down in an upright position. Our backs were pressed to the lower side of the slanted wall, with our feet and hands pressed awkwardly against the other side. We lurched ourselves forward, grunting with each motion. We laughed at first at the sheer awkwardness of our movements, but we fell silent soon after. We'd only gone about fifteen feet and we were exhausted.

The first few sections were so narrow, our arms were fixed in the lower half of a push-up position, unable to extend them out any farther. If I attempted to turn my face forward, I'd scrape the skin from the tip of my nose. "Resting" could only be achieved by inhaling deeply until our rib cages wedged in between the two walls, allowing our feet to dangle. Every thirty or forty feet, the cracks would open into sandy chambers wide enough for us to stretch our arms out and not much else.

It was as though we were moving through the bowels of a beast, slipping slowly from one cavity to the next. Inside each chamber, we'd reconvene. Bucket and Dagwood would move back and forth between them, only able to turn around and go back once they'd reached an opening. After a few hours, they began to grow anxious at our inability to move at their pace. We'd hear their whining echoing off the walls in disorienting patterns, as if they were above us and behind us and below us. They'd dash ahead and then reappear in front of us, excitedly, before realizing they couldn't turn around and now needed to shuffle backward until the crack opened up into the next chamber before righting themselves.

I wouldn't describe myself as claustrophobic, but after the third hour, I longed for just one deep breath. One breath that wasn't grated with sand on the inhale. Neil was out in front of me when I heard him shout, "It's opening up!"

Within a few feet, I was finally able to walk facing forward for the first time since we'd climbed in. My neck was stiff, my knees were bloodied, and the back of my shirt was ripped open and soaked with sweat. Before us, an unusually large chamber, about eight feet in height, but long and rounded like a tunnel with muddy water up to our ankles.

The dogs frolicked about, thrilled at the expanse of this particular room, as Neil and I dropped our packs onto a patch of dry sand and collapsed. "We've got to be almost there," he said, between bites of a smashed granola bar. "This is the big open section, so there should just be some short sections ahead with high stemming."

I couldn't help but laugh at the idea that this cave we sat in was "the big open section." At the roof of the subway tunnel, the opening in the rock shrunk back down to just a few inches wide and remained that narrow clear up to the blue sky fifty feet above. The only way a human being could fit through there would be if they'd been turned to rainwater. After we'd huffed down two granola bars each and a gallon of water, our spirits were lifted.

Descriptions for slot canyons can be futile, often laughable. We were entering volatile and ever-changing cracks in the ground based on information someone wrote about it years, or even decades, ago. Sometimes descriptions contained such comical vagaries as "Look for the big rock" or "Exit near a tree on your left." The fact that we had reached such a large and unmistakable landmark as the subway tunnel let us know exactly where we were amid the generalized description. It couldn't be much longer now.

We repacked our bags and called for the dogs, who had chased a lizard into the crack we'd just come from. They reappeared, muddied and panting. Up ahead, as expected, the glorious expanse of the subway tunnel shrunk once again. Forty feet from where it started, our shoulders were once again pressed flush to sandstone.

I paused in a place wide enough to face forward and removed my camera from the protective pouch in my backpack. I fumbled with the exposure, trying to capture the right amount of light, the detail in the rock. When I rounded the corner, Neil's motionless back was to me. He stood, staring straight ahead at the tapering crack as it narrowed to no more than six inches wide. We couldn't possibly fit through that. The dogs couldn't even fit through it. They pawed at the sand restlessly, their whining adding to the growing sense of panic.

"What the fuck is that, Neil?!" He didn't answer. He was staring at the ripped-out piece of paper from the guidebook in his hands as if there was something we'd missed, as if it might suddenly grow wings and carry us out. He turned to me and said, "This must be the high-stemming portion."

We'd known this was coming. High stemming is a common obstacle in technical canyons. It involves climbing well above the canyon floor by pressing upward with our back, hands, feet, knees, or anything else that spans the width of the walls. This is necessary when it's too narrow to squeeze through at the ground level, forcing us to climb up and over the constriction in the rock. Oftentimes, we needed to press our way up thirty feet or more, rendering even the slightest slip deadly.

We had high stemmed over narrow sections before, but we'd never encountered one so narrow that the dogs couldn't shimmy through beneath us. For the first time in the history of this bizarre hobby we had taken up, we had no idea how to get them out.

I collapsed onto the sand in the small opening before the inevitable up-climb. There was no way to go back. That was the thing about canyoneering. We move through the rock the way water does, rolling and tumbling down and down and down until eventually we're spit out of a crack in the wall into a larger canyon wash. Once we committed to the maze of sandstone plumbing, the only way out was through.

Neil sat across from me with our knees touching, the dogs lying at our sides, licking the heavy mud from their paws. He looked upward, seeming to silently weigh the options of climbing all the way up. If he could climb out, he could make it back to the van. Perhaps he could get a longer rope, find something to build an anchor off of, haul us out before it got too dark. Or perhaps he'd fall, careening down through those narrow walls, landing in a broken heap right on top of us.

I didn't think my heart could survive watching him stem precariously up softened rock. Even if he did make it safely to the top, it would mean he would disappear beyond the edge, and I'd be alone, waiting.

The fear was compounded exponentially by the guilt. I had led my dogs into the unknown. We would have never let anything happen to them, but the reality of the situation was that if something happened to us, something *would* happen to them. They'd be stuck in that canyon. The idea was paralyzing, excruciating, to think we had failed them like that. We had to get them out, which meant we had to get ourselves out.

After weighing all of our options, we decided we had no choice but to keep going. By some miraculous feat of strength, we would each need to attach one dog to our harness and hoist them upward more than thirty feet to traverse sideways through this section, which we had no idea the actual length of.

Neil made the first run through with his backpack dangling from his harness between his legs. Through grunts and gasps, he called back his progress. Forty feet. Fifty feet. Sixty feet. By the time he reached the next chamber, I could hardly make out what he was saying. He dropped the backpack and stemmed all the way back to where I stood waiting with the dogs. I carefully tightened all four leg loops on their harnesses as Neil tethered them to our harnesses with locking carabiners. Neil would take Dagwood. I would follow closely behind with Bucket.

Neil dug his knees into one wall and slid his bare back up the other. Dagwood lifted a whole three inches off the ground and now hung level, but confused, between Neil's legs. The veins in Neil's forehead were bulging, sweat seeping from every pore as he slid up inch after agonizing inch. Once he was high enough to begin traversing over, he paused to reach down and adjust Dags, who still hung beneath him like a piñata.

I pressed my hands to the wall in front of me and my back to the one behind and pushed upward as hard as I could. Bucket and I did not move an inch. After several deep breaths, I pressed again, harder this time, and lifted us ever so slightly out of the mud. We held our position for no more than ten seconds before crashing back down in a mess of paws and feet.

I changed my strategy. I dug my bony knee into the wall in front of me and pressed my hands downward behind me. Letting out a series of primal screams, I managed to get us up about twenty feet before bursting into tears. Neil shouted words of encouragement as he disappeared around the corner with Dagwood swinging below. For his sake, he couldn't stop to help us.

Suddenly my palms, soaked with sweat, slipped from the sandstone behind me and sent the back of my skull crashing into the wall. My knees began to slide slowly down the opposite wall, leaving two perfect trails of dark blood like paint. Below me was Bucket and below Bucket was a V-shaped crack that would shatter any limb that fell into it. I screamed Neil's name. I screamed every swear word I could think of. The nearest cell phone service was over three hours away from the crack I was now wedged inside of in a half-upside-down fetal position.

By the time Neil had gotten Dagwood through and scrambled back to me, my screaming had turned to hyperventilating. I could feel the blood dripping down my back, dripping down my calves, dripping onto Bucket's back.

"Help me!" I cried as Neil's face appeared above mine. He slid down beneath me ever-so-slightly, propping Bucket up on one of his legs, effectively removing her sixty pounds of weight from my harness. With a swift motion, he clipped her carabiner to himself and took her from me. I righted myself and dragged my bloodied body behind him as he grunted his way through the walls.

When we made it around the corner, Dagwood leapt from the sand to greet us. With all four of Bucket's paws back on the ground, I collapsed in a heap and sobbed. Neil grabbed my cheeks in his hands and pressed his forehead to mine.

"What the fuck are we doing?!" I shrieked. "This is fucking insane."

"I know, I know, I know," he whispered over and over into my sweaty mess of hair. It seemed like forever that we sat there holding each other, rocking back and forth in the dampened dark, before Neil spoke.

"We set a check-in time with Mark and Steve. If they don't hear from us by Monday night, they'll know to send search and rescue."

"Neil," I said quietly, staring at Bucket and Dagwood asleep against our legs, "... it's Saturday."

The reality was, we did not have enough food or water for the four of us to wait that long. The more crushing reality was, it would be my fault if we were tucked between frigid rock walls as the sun disappeared and the black night crept in. Spiders would descend their silken ropes around us; rats would emerge from bundles of sticks lodged above our heads, the night-green glow of their eyes brighter than any moon. And we would lie there among them, frigid and out of place, all because I wasn't strong enough.

And so, I was faced with a decision as old as time itself. Give up or go forward. The only way out was through.

We spent the next hour traversing through more high-stemming sections, pressing our open wounds into the walls over and over and over, biting little holes in our own cheeks to distract from the pain everywhere else. For every section I passed through, Neil went back and forth through it three times. I felt absolutely useless.

Eventually, a narrow section tapered into a small sand opening, as it had so many times that day, and the four of us curled up there and shared the last granola bar. Neil reached over and gathered me up in his arms, whispering words of encouragement into the limp form my body had taken.

When I lifted my eyes to look beyond the mess of his tangled hair, Bucket lay in a small circular patch of sun, eyes closed in bliss. It was practically blinding to stare into, but we couldn't help but notice that it seemed to be beaming onto her from the side.

We clambered over one another, and through the cloud of sand kicked up in the frenzy, a bright white crack appeared before us. I held my breath as my eyes adjusted, and then I saw it. A tree. One single green tree flooded in sunlight. We had reached the end.

Bursting through the final squeeze, we lowered the dogs on a short rope before losing patience and leaping six feet down into a thick pile of mud that had oozed from the slot like blood. We lurched forward onto dry sand and crumpled, awash in adrenaline, rife with blood, staring up into the spinning blue sky. Six hours after we'd climbed in, we climbed back out.

I don't know how long we lay there. All I know is that the blood all over my body had dried completely by the time I next lifted my head. Bucket was fast asleep, pressed against my side, digging out little trenches of sand with each puff from her nostrils. Dagwood had curled up beneath the shade of the singular cottonwood tree that stood proudly over the desolation of the wash like Lady Liberty.

None of us moved until the sun dipped behind one of the walls. For a moment, I thought perhaps I'd only dreamt that we'd gotten out. The visceral warmth of the sun on my skin was the only sure thing I knew. I rolled over and curled up into Neil's neck, breathing in the dried sweat and the powdered-sugar particles of sand, knowing how far deep I would still be in that crack if not for him.

Eventually, we limped our way back to the van, tore open a bottle of whiskey, and drank it dry. I bit down on the cork as Neil swiped an alcohol swab over my battered knees. The following morning, we awoke to find the bedsheets cemented into our newly formed scabs.

We had squeezed our way through the walls of that canyon in much the same way we had squeezed through the past few years of our lives together. Enthusiastic and brazen, despite all the times we'd barely made it out. We always seemed to find each other, to rely on each other in the chaos, but sometimes only after doubling back in order to do so. We began making plans in separate locations, dreaming on different timelines. I would have maps ready and the van packed for the moment Neil's shifts were over, ushering him up into the driver's seat of Bertha so *my* adventure could begin.

He would nod and smile and follow along, but I wonder now, did I ask him if that's what he wanted? Did he ever tell me he didn't? Did I not listen, or did he not speak? I suppose it doesn't always make a difference. In the end, those who say nothing can be just as culpable as those who say too much.

PART III

A ship is safe in harbor, but that is not what ships are built for.

—JOHN A. SHEDD

My bright yellow rain boots looked out of place strapped to a stretcher. The ambulance driver said it was protocol that I had to ride that way, even though my injuries were strictly internal. Not internal like organ damage or bone fractures. Internal like not getting out of bed for weeks. Internal like stockpiling prescription sleeping pills wrapped in an old T-shirt under my dorm room mattress.

By the time I went to college, it had been just over six years since I'd spoken to my father. I knew that anger was killing me, but I couldn't let go of it. I had built so much of my identity on it. A beautiful, yet tortured short story I wrote about my youth and my father was what had won me a local nonfiction writing contest and a small college scholarship. I was convinced *grief* was what made me a writer, and I was too afraid to find out what I might be without it. So, I slid, headlong, into my clichéd version of what it meant to be a "tortured artist." I stopped taking my antidepressants, stopped eating, stopped going to classes. Neil and I broke up in a fiery, screaming phone call because he said he just couldn't understand this haunted shadow of the person I'd become. He was in college. He wanted to have fun. He didn't want to listen to the monotone dragging of my lifeless voice on the other end of the phone day after day. Who could blame him?

So, with Neil gone and my grades plummeting and my clothes sliding down the shoulders of my skeletal frame, there was only one thing left to do to complete my self-sabotage. I stopped sleeping. I stared at my ceiling and blared music into my headphones and sobbed into my pillow. I'd call my mother at all hours of the night and scream into the phone in unintelligible gasps. She was hours away in Connecticut, helpless as I withered away inside the walls I had built for myself. Out of desperation, she did the only thing she could think to do. She called a family friend—a doctor—and asked him to write me a prescription for sleeping pills. If I could just get some sleep, she figured, then everything else might fall into place. Perhaps I'd be able to eat or go to class or go to work or appear even remotely human for half a day.

After stopping at the pharmacy on campus, I sat on my bed staring at the bottle of Ambien for a good long while before I swallowed one. Then another, for good measure. It was ten o'clock in the morning, but I hadn't really considered that. I awoke fourteen hours later, in the middle of the night, fully dressed on top of my red quilt. Once the disorientation wore off, the relief set in. I had been freed from all those hours. There in the darkness, I placed two more pills in my mouth and curled back up beneath an old sweatshirt. Climbing under the blankets was too exhausting to even consider. The way I saw it, the next time I opened my eyes, I would have skipped an entire day.

It took only a few weeks for my body to adjust to the Ambien. First two pills would put me out for a whole day, but then I needed three. Soon my roommates reported that I was up and walking around, smashing into walls and tripping down stairs as if I were drunk. I'd mumble nonsense at them and then wander back into my room and sleep for another six hours without any memory of having even been "awake" in the first place. When they told me what I'd done, how I'd come staggering into the kitchen like a zombie, it terrified me. Not enough to stop, of course, but enough to start taking four pills a day. Then five. There's no way I'd be able to wander around then. It would just be like I was dead, I thought. That's the statement that sealed my fate in the college counseling office a few weeks later. My roommates had begged me to go. They thought it would be good for me to talk to someone. I watched the clinician straighten up after I said the word *dead*. "Do you have a plan?" she asked. I thought about telling her how I'd begun to obsess over thoughts of writing a letter to my father, and leaping off a pier into the Atlantic in the depths of winter. But that seemed too grisly to say out loud. Instead, I offered up the fact that I'd been stockpiling prescription pills beneath my mattress. The ambulance arrived twenty-five minutes later.

I was committed to a state-run inpatient psychiatric unit, sharing a room with a woman from Providence who ate all the staples from the magazines my mom brought during visiting hours. My mom hadn't noticed. She was busy demanding that the staff use their employee fridge to store the almond milk she had brought me from Whole Foods.

Most of my days I spent sleeping, leaving my room only for mandatory group therapy, pill distribution, and one-on-one meetings with my assigned doctor. She was a striking Indian woman who sat stoically across from me as I mocked my own presence in this place. The women who roamed these halls in backless hospital gowns and Trazodone-induced fogs had been raped. They'd been molested, beaten, attacked. They'd battled drug addictions for years. The state had taken away their children. They screamed at night because they believed the ceiling was crawling. And here I was, some middle-class college student with daddy issues and a mother out in the hallway arguing about milk alternatives.

"It's laughable," I scoffed, but the doctor wasn't laughing. She returned to the notepad on the desk in front of her.

"Is there a history of suicide in your family?"

"No," I lied.

"Have you ever attempted suicide or had serious thoughts of suicide before?"

"No," I lied.

"That's not what you told the counselor at the student center," she said, completely unenthused with my bullshit. She lifted her head, pen still poised to the page. I stared at her blankly.

"It's a habit of yours, isn't it? To belittle your own pain? To constantly compare it to others as a way to justify ignoring it? You don't deserve to be here because you're not *as* sick or *as* sad. Do you think you'll be thinking about anyone else's pain the day you put all those pills in your mouth? Or the day Lola isn't in the car with you?"

My head shot up. "Lola?" I asked.

"Tell me about Christmas last year," she said, staring directly at me for what felt like the first time. I had entirely forgotten that I mumbled that story out to the counselor back at campus. Ambien will do that sometimes.

After a long silence, I looked up at the doctor and whispered, "The lights were immaculate . . ."

My mom had moved in with her second husband in a town called Westport. It was by far the nicest neighborhood she had ever lived in. The trim of his old white colonial dripped with soft white lights like icicles; a fresh green wreath and a bright red bow in every window. Beneath each one, a small battery-powered candle. I recognized them as the ones my mother put in every window of our little blue house each Christmas for as long as I could remember. I pulled in the driveway after the three-and-a-half-hour drive home, a heaping sack of dirty laundry on the front seat. Sitting in the road with my blinker still clicking, I could picture my mom on a stepladder with armfuls of evergreen, lights twinkling around her like a halo.

My depression had been getting worse. The essays I wrote for my classes were all rambling, heartbroken homages to abandonment. I couldn't let go of the feeling of my dad leaving. In fact, it was hardly a *feeling* at all. It was deeper than that, somehow. It lived in my body, on a molecular level. Something always felt . . . missing. It was woven into the very fabric of who I was, of how I saw myself.

When I arrived at her house, my mother followed me nervously, making sure I wasn't sneaking wine bottles up to the guest room or fashioning a noose out of a string of lights. But after a while, her surveillance waned. On Christmas night, after drinking a fair amount of said stolen wine, I took her car keys and snuck out the side door with the aging family Chihuahua, Lola, tucked under one arm and another unopened bottle of wine under the other. Earlier that week, I had run into an old acquaintance at the supermarket who casually mentioned that she drove by my dad's house all the time. "Couldn't miss that big truck if you tried," she said, "right in his driveway off Route 58!" She was so cheerfully and obviously unaware that I had no idea what that house looked like, that I hadn't seen that truck since I was sixteen.

I waited until I had rounded the corner to turn the car's headlights on and then I drove silently through the dark toward Route 58. The houses up there were old colonials with big front porches and sprawling yards, shrouded in trees so tall and thick the night seemed vacuous. I cracked the window to look up at the sliver of stars. When I was a kid, my family would attend Christmas Eve midnight mass every year. On the rides home, my brother and I would bounce in our seats, swearing we would stay up late enough this time to catch Santa. My dad would be singing some carol in a funny accent from the driver's seat. Mom would ask if I could see any reindeer in the sky.

A dusting of snow-turned-ice remained on the grass, reflecting the lights of reindeer statues and inflatable waving Santa Clauses. Driveways were packed with cars. Bay window after bay window glowed with fireplaces and Christmas trees and candlelit tables surrounded by families. Only once or twice did I see someone distracted enough to notice the strange car idling out in the road, the strange girl squinting over the steering wheel at each truck in the driveway.

For a long time, I tried to convince myself that I had just gone for a late-night drive. It was too difficult to admit that I'd brought a bottle of wine in case I did find his house . . . in case he and his wife and stepdaughters did invite me in. It was too difficult to admit that I'd brought Lola on my lap in case I didn't find his house . . . in case I needed one tiny, innocent reason not to jerk the wheel and plow the whole car into a tree.

Years later I did find his house. In the early stages of our efforts to reconcile, he invited me over for dinner with him and his wife. Neil and I had gotten back together a few months after I'd left the hospital and had been together ever since. He squeezed my hand tightly from the driver's seat as we turned, once again, onto Route 58. When we pulled into the driveway, I recognized it as one of the houses I had driven by that night. My breath caught in my chest. I fanned my eyes so as not to ruin my mascara. Neil and I each took a swig from an open beer can in the cup holder. Inside, we hugged awkwardly and idled near the doorway. Too many of us were trying to say too many things at once. I held out a bottle of red wine to my dad's wife like an altar offering. It was organic, from a local vineyard. I'd spent nearly half an hour pacing back and forth in front of the rack at a wine store no twenty-one-year-old had any business shopping in. "Organic" was the only word I kept reiterating to the salesperson. I couldn't very well show up with a box of the cheap shit my friends and I gulped down on weekends. The bottle I settled on must have been almost seventy dollars.

When I handed it to her, she inspected the label before announcing, abruptly, that she couldn't drink it. Something about sulfites. I wish she had just pretended that she could. I wish she had just taken it and regifted it to someone else the next day. So, I stood clutching it to my chest, embarrassed, as they began a tour of the house. Their instruments, their matching snakeskin cowboy boots, some custom paintings they had done. We sidestepped down a hallway, the walls covered in photographs. Not a single one was of me or my brother. My dad pointed to one with a gold frame that seemed to glow in the light from the fireplace. It was one of his stepdaughters onstage at a ballet recital in a crisp white tutu, toe poised perfectly to the sky. He stood back and smiled. "That's Kristina. That's my little ballerina girl."

All I remember after that was my hand, sweating, clutching the back of a leather armchair as the room grew smaller. They had continued down the wall, pointing at photos of their cats and their band onstage at a show, but I stood frozen. Neil knew. He kept his hand firmly on my lower back, practically pushing to keep me upright. I wanted to wrap my fist around the neck of that wine bottle and smash it against the wall; shatter the glass and watch the photo inside melt over in bloodred Merlot on the hardwood floor. It came out so flippantly, so naturally to him. Something he just mentioned in passing. But it was the most painful thing anyone has ever said to me.

I had driven right past his house that Christmas night with tears blurring my vision, Lola pressed to my chest. Right past the cozy fireplace and the Christmas tree and the exquisite, glowing picture of the ballerina girl. I just wanted to understand something that I still don't to this day. I just wanted someone to tell me why I was in the dark, and she was in a frame.

Hours must have gone by before the doctor told me our time was up. But she knew this was the most honest I had ever been, and I knew our time had been up a long time ago. The way it came out in choking gasps and half-thoughts; the way I retched it up like vomit. There was no semblance of the beautiful essays I read out in class. It was just the truth, clawing its way up through my bowels, weaving through my rib cage like black oil and spilling out onto the desk.

"Brianna," she said finally, "you are here because your 'check engine' light came on six years ago when your father left. And you just kept driving. Of course you broke down." She leaned over the desk, patted the top of my hand with hers, and said it once more. "Of course you broke down."

Back in my room, I lay staring at the barren branches, the way they swayed with the stiffness of winter. They tapped almost rhythmically against the steel bars that covered all the windows. Of course I had broken down. I had truly believed that turning the radio up loud enough or rolling all the windows down would drown out the sound of all the parts beneath the hood hanging on by a thread, and then seizing, and then dying. I couldn't ignore it anymore. Despite how attached I had grown to the grief; I would have to let it go if I didn't want to die.

If you seek out struggle, you must not really know it. I hear versions of this all the time. *If you live as though you've nothing to lose, you must never have lost anything.* But that is rarely the case. In fact, I don't know anyone who does risky things with the hope that they won't survive them. However, I know plenty of people who do risky things because they've already survived the things that were supposed to be safest of all. Childhoods that were promised to be idyllic and love that was promised to be unconditional.

By the time I moved into a van in the desert, I cared more about living a wild life than a long one. I took huge risks—sometimes resulting in huge consequences—but there had seldom been a moment when it didn't feel worth it. People clucked their tongues at me because I lived differently; even dangerously in their eyes. But I refused to coddle myself with the belief that conventional choices were better, because conventional choices would keep me safe. I knew bad things could happen to anyone, because bad things happen to everyone. People die every day. They die in extreme sports accidents and accidents on the way to their office. Some people get a sudden, terminal diagnosis. Some people die trying to sail oceans, summit mountains. Some people's beloved dogs slip their collars, dig a hole under the fence, and run out into the street. Some people keel over, stone-dead, while tending to the rose garden in their front yard.

I didn't want a rose garden. I wanted a story to tell, no matter what risks it would require to tell it.

The sacred datura, or moon lily, is an ethereal, velvet-leaved white flower that grows in the rocky soil at the base of desert cliffs. Trumpeted blossoms with lavender-tinged edges open only at night, when they glow a cool blue, as if made of ice. Navajo shamans were known to brew tea from this plant, which would induce in its drinkers a stronger hallucinogenic experience than either LSD or peyote. The wrong amount is fatal, but the right amount produces paralysis of the parasympathetic nervous system, shaking, sweating, fever, hallucinations, and acute psychosis. My mother was certain I had made a large cup of this tea for myself when I called her to tell her I was quitting my job.

"Brianna Elizabeth, have you been drinking moon lily again?"

I suppose she should have no longer been surprised by my sporadic voicemails outlining plans to live in a car, or disappear into Mexico, or start collecting ball pythons, or run off and join the circus. She had held her breath each time I'd leapt and applauded each time I landed, but never without voicing her opinion first. And her opinion on the matter of me quitting my well-paying job with benefits and a 401(k) to go sit in a van in the desert and write stories on Instagram? A resounding no.

In my mother's defense, this brilliant idea of quitting my job *had* come to me after hearing an Alan Watts speech from the 1960s about the philosophy of life during a weekend of tripping on mushrooms in the desert. I won't transcribe the whole thing for brevity's sake, but let's just say Watts equates life not with a journey, but with music. The point of music is not to get to the end, and the point of dancing is not to get to one place in the room. "We thought of life by analogy with a pilgrimage, which had a serious purpose at that end, and the thing was to *get* to that end. Success, or whatever it is, or maybe heaven after you're dead," he says. "But we missed the point the whole way along. It was a musical thing, and you were supposed to sing or to dance while the music was being played."

Now, when I was tripping on mushrooms and the sky had waves like the ocean and the yucca looked like crowns of fallen kings and my skin was tingling all over, those words were like religion. As in most psychedelic experiences, the thought of up and leaving my job seemed brilliant and profound at the time, and outright absurd in the aftermath. Like taking a glassy-eyed journey to a beautiful oasis, only to come down and realize I was just high on a public beach.

Despite all this, I spent the following Monday pacing back and forth in my office as Bucket and Dagwood slept under the desk. I knew that if I was going to do this, I would have to do it quick. I had spent enough time standing at the edge of cliffs to know that I could not hesitate. The longer you stand at the top of something, the less likely you are to jump off. I sat on the floor and stared across the office at my desk, eye-level with my shower caddy, the purple loofah still dripping from that morning's shower. *I don't know where the fuck I'm gonna take a shower*, I suddenly realized. One would think I would be weighing the price of losing third-party health insurance or working an Excel budget spreadsheet, but mainly I was just concerned with where I would find free hot water to thaw my frozen extremities. The *pings* of frantic incoming emails reverberated off the walls of my office. I fantasized about how little that sound would mean to me someday; how much it had meant to me for the last two years.

I took a deep breath and walked upstairs to my boss's office. I hadn't quite thought of what I planned to say to him, but it scarcely mattered, as I spent the first five minutes weeping anyway. When I finally managed to explain that I had to quit, he politely asked, "And why is that?"

"I don't know, I just have to!" I practically shouted back.

I paused for a moment to consider how manic I was sounding, but it was the only answer I had. I was quitting because I just had to. Something told me I had to. Perhaps it was that crackly recording of Alan Watts, or the palmful of mushrooms I'd swallowed with peanut butter. Or perhaps those had simply cleared the thick fog that can fill one's brain after the comfort of routine sets in.

A week later, I plopped a small cardboard box onto the front seat of the van. My toiletries from the basement bathroom, some unused notepads, and a few framed photos were all I walked out of my office with. I would have kept my beloved desk plant if I weren't certain it would be dead within days. I made a few stops around Salt Lake City before swinging by my storage unit to pack. I wouldn't be going to an office down the block each week, so I needed to increase my supply of belongings in the van.

Bucket and Dagwood chased each other down the long corridors as I tossed clothes and backpacks over my shoulders onto one of the complimentary carts. I was still overcome with a tremendous sense of urgency. I had to get out of town as fast as possible lest I panic and go slinking back to my office, begging for my job back. If I was still here, I could still change my mind.

As I drove south out of the bounds of the city and up the canyon road that had been spitting me into the desert weekend after weekend after weekend, it suddenly dawned on me that I didn't ever *have* to go back. There were no payments, no meetings, no appointments, no presentations or due dates. Sunday night was not coming for me. I had tossed my only anchor overboard, cut my tether to the rocket, and watched from a black vacuum void as it drifted off without me.

Out there on that highway, I was free. That windows-down kind of free I'd seen in movies and heard about in classic rock songs. The kind of free that should have made me feel a long-awaited sense of joy, and yet the only thing I could muster was terror.

I skidded half-violently onto the gravel shoulder, just shy of the summit pass, on the road that would drop me down into the desert I was so certain I belonged in. Passing tractor trailers shifted Bertha on her tires with forceful gusts. I stared ahead blankly, engine idling. Bucket and Dagwood leapt from the bed in the back and began circling the front seats, peering at me curiously. *Why have we stopped? Where are we going? What now?*

I don't know.

My breathing quickened as I dropped my head to the steering wheel. I let out a gasp, followed by a heaving sob, as if I'd been holding my breath for hours. Holding in the terror that lay trapped beneath the puffed-up chest of someone who'd just left everything behind. What if I had made a terrible mistake? My only plan was to start using the small but devoted popularity I had gained on Instagram and the meager, sporadic income I made from advertising products to take some time off and focus on myself. I hoped this brief freedom from an office job would offer me a burst of clarity on what exactly I wanted to do with my life. Neil had been the one to pose the practical questions: What if Instagram income wasn't enough to cover Bertha's gas? Where would I get my health insurance? What if I walked away from everything and in its place found nothing?

All my life, I'd assumed it was only brave people who did brave things. I'd never once considered how many of them were absolutely terrified.

Several weeks after I quit my job, my mother flew from Connecticut to Utah to spend a week in the van with me. Neil busied himself at work so we girls would have some time to ourselves.

Having no air-conditioning wasn't something I ever thought about until someone else was subjected to a couple of hours in the van. My mother fanned herself with a book as we drove out of the airport and along the Wasatch mountain range. In the deep summer, I was known to drive in nothing but underwear and a tank top with a beach towel beneath me on the seat. By the time I arrived anywhere, there were always two perfectly thigh-shaped prints of sweat beneath me.

I planned to take my mother camping in a place called the Swell. It was a vast stretch of public land close to Neil's field office. I knew it like the back of my hand, having spent every weekend there for nearly two years by then.

I pulled into a gas station in the last one-light town before pavement turned to dirt. Mom ran inside to use the restroom as I gassed up and lifted the hood to check on Bertha's shiny new radiator. The previous one had started sprouting fluid on a rocky pass on the outskirts of Escalante a few weeks back. There on the side of the road, Neil taught me how to crack eggs from our cooler and pour the whites into the radiator to temporarily plug the leak.

The gas pump clicked and spat out a faded receipt as my mother jumped back up into the van. I watched as she peered out the window at the trailer homes and desolate storefronts. Casualties of small-town life. Ranchers with pickup trucks full of herding dogs would stop in the middle of the road to have a chat with their neighbors. Child-sized dirt bikes lay keeled over in gravel driveways. Despite the broiling summer temperatures, some houses still bore plastic, sun-faded Christmas decorations. My mother winced at the sight.

We turned left past a field of horses and wild mule deer grazing alongside each other. I wondered if the horses ever felt sad watching the deer leap over the fence and out of sight while they remained tethered to that one place.

Bertha kicked up dust as the road grew narrower, the near-forgotten little town disappearing behind us. Juniper trees rose up around large clearings full of cows, their babies frolicking along behind them with surprising agility. Cheatgrass and rabbitbrush lined the road, though they had been coated over with dust from passing trucks. If my mother lived there, I imagine she would have jumped from the van to clean them off, to replant any that the cattle may have trampled. That was her way—to grow things even in unlikely places.

At the final intersection, I looked over and asked, "You ready, Mama?" She bounced in her seat as I pulled straight up the edge of

Utah's version of the Grand Canyon. Only here, there were no gift shops or parking areas. In fact, the only thing to keep cars from driving straight over the 1,200-foot edge, Thelma-and-Louise-style, was a little line of boulders.

I hooked a left and drove farther along the edge of the canyon, my mother's face pressed to the window on the right. She barely waited for me to put it in park before leaping from the front seat. Bucket and Dagwood followed her out the door and disappeared, as they always did.

I began busying about, setting our campsite up and arranging a clean blanket over a chair for my mom. Behind me, she stood at the panoramic edge of the canyon with both hands clasped over her mouth. The view was dramatic, breathtaking, unlike anything she had seen in her life. And I had brought her here. I swelled with pride standing beside her, pointing out the tiny river at the bottom that was responsible for this deeply cut canyon. I pointed to various spires and buttes, reciting their names and the types of sandstone they were made of. Navajo and Wingate and Kayenta formations. Layers of rock forty to seventy million years old.

"And to think after all that time, here we are . . ." she whispered, breathless.

With the sun setting, I cooked pasta and asparagus on the Coleman stove while my mom looked on from the raggedy red chair I'd set up for her. I suddenly felt embarrassed by the months' worth of crusted food that coated the surface beneath the burners. A dirty camp stove is a rite of passage in most outdoor circles, but it doesn't tend to go over as well with mothers. To her credit, she made no mention of it, though I did catch her meticulously scrubbing the spoon I handed her with the bottom corner of her shirt.

We dragged our chairs out to the ledge with dinner plates on our laps, watching the dogs shuffle down sloping talus hillsides on the scent of big-horned sheep.

When we'd finished, I showed her how I summoned the black-winged bats by tossing pebbles straight up into the sky at dusk. They'd swoop in, assuming it was a horsefly or a juicy moth. When we were camped near sparse desert water sources and the mosquitoes were out, Neil and I would toss up pebbles like mad to bring the bats. "Calling in reinforcements," we'd say.

Back at camp, I demonstrated how to pluck small bunches of juniper bristles and use them as a natural scrubber to clean the pots and pans. "Leaves a nice scent too!" I smiled proudly. With classical music playing from my portable speaker, we unfolded a bouldering crash pad and laid it out right in the center of the road we'd driven in on. Out here, there was rarely a need to worry about other cars.

We took turns taking pulls from a bottle of Malbec I had brought home from Argentina as the velvet night swooped in and the last of the sunset turned purple, then black. Overhead, we pointed out shooting stars and satellites—or were they passing planes? Whatever they were, they were very, very far away. When "Clair de Lune" started drifting softly from the speaker, we fell silent, breathing in and out, pressed up against each other in the dirt.

There were plenty of ways I wanted to be like my mother and plenty of ways that I didn't. I wondered if she knew that. How could she not? She had flown 2,300 miles to the mountains and then been driven four hours into the depths of the desert so that I could show her the strange little life I'd made; a life that was nothing like hers. If she was at all hurt by that, she never showed it.

But I suppose that's what they say about parents. They usually want their children to go out and become all the things they never thought to be, do all the things they didn't think they could.

Despite everything, I suspect I turned out more like my mother than either of us thought. I had taken those slivers of naked liberation she had shown me and woven a whole life out of them. I was who I was now both in spite of her and because of her.

The next morning, after a breakfast of eggs and coffee, I set up a tripod and a self-timer to capture what would ultimately become an all-time favorite photo of mine. Mom and I on the bed beneath the blankets, our heads pressed together and poking out from the van's back doors, smiling widely.

Years later, my brother and I were called to come before a notary who was overseeing some adjustments my mother was making to her living will. She is organized to a fault, constantly making sure I know all of her passwords and the locations of files scattered throughout various storage units. She was transferring power of attorney to me, should any medical decisions need to be made on her behalf.

The notary flipped each page, pointing to various lines for signatures and initials. On one of the final pages, my pen hovered just above the signature line as I read and reread the clause. My mother had written: *I hereby request that my body be cremated, and that my ashes be scattered by my only daughter, should she survive me, at the overlook of the Wedge in Utah.*

There was nothing in every direction. The kind of nothing you can only understand if you've seen that kind of nothing before. An hour north of Lusk, Wyoming—a couple hundred cornfields from the borders of South Dakota and Nebraska—Bertha sat disemboweled and steaming on a gravel mining road, her bright orange paint a singular blemish on the vacant horizon.

Neil lay on the dirt beside the front axle with one huge tire flat on the ground beside him and a collection of rusted tools scattered around his body like funeral flowers. Through the front passenger window, Bucket and Dagwood stared down at him, keeping vigil.

The only thing that disrupted all that nothingness was the tornado of dirt-road dust that came tearing in from the east on the heels of a coal truck an hour later. The dogs were barking mad by the time the squealing of the engine brake reached us. When the dust settled, I stood staring up at a gaunt, gray-skinned man with a cigarette hanging from his lips. He chuckled at the sight of me, as most small-town locals did, and said flatly, "You're a long ways from home, huh?"

It was the fall of 2017 and I was trying to make this whole not-having-a-job thing work, so I accepted a paid gig with the South Dakota Department of Tourism. They signed me on to drive Bertha roughly seven hundred miles up from the deserts of Utah to the southwest corner of South Dakota to document a weeklong trip through some outdoor attractions.

Being that posting and advertising were my full-time "job" now, I accepted. Now, it should not be understated that agreeing to drive a notoriously unpredictable vehicle with over 260,000 miles on it for thirteen hours through the night was brazen at best, and absolutely idiotic at worst. But we'd never been to South Dakota. Not only did we have the chance to go see a new place, but we were actually getting *paid* to do it. So, on a Thursday evening, once Neil had finished work, we loaded Bucket and Dagwood into the van and headed north through the night toward rolling stretches of Wyoming freeway. We listened to playlists and podcasts and stopped around 2:00 a.m. to sleep for a few hours in a cold Walmart parking lot before rising with the sun to continue.

Some twenty miles outside of Casper, Wyoming, we began breathing in the first hints of hot metal and burning oil. When you drive an old vehicle and you start to smell something *mechanical* there's always a dreadful internal battle that takes place. *Do I pull over immediately, or do I carry on, hoping the problem belongs to some schmuck in the passing lane?*

Within the next eight hundred feet, the smell became so pungent it practically stung our eyes. We pulled onto the shoulder beside a field of sunflowers and sat for a moment as tractor trailers blew past, rocking Bertha violently each time. I rolled my window down and leaned out to find torrents of smoke billowing from the front passenger tire. Squatting next to the oil-spattered rubber, Neil reached out slowly to touch the hub, winced, and snapped his fingers back. The metal was hot enough to blister skin. Neil sent out a series of expletives as he lay on the ground beneath the front axle. He sat up through the smoke and announced, "It's basically like a grenade went off inside our wheel bearing."

I walked down the freeway shoulder with my hands on my head before turning back toward the smoking pile of orange metal. Staring at her from a bit of a distance now, I realized that the tire in question was not only smoking, but also leaning inward at the top, as though the weight of the van was melting it into the pavement.

"The whole fucking tire is gonna fall off, Neil!" I said in disbelief over the roar of passing motorists.

The front axle had started giving us trouble back near Lander, and no shop within a hundred miles had a replacement spindle for a custom-built 1990 Ford E350 with an axle ripped off a 1979 Ford F150. We had begged and borrowed every mile out of her since. Years of teetering on the edge of adventure and disaster had provided Neil and me with the type of last-ditch optimism that led us to say things like "Maybe it's not that bad," or "Maybe we can just make it twenty more miles," or "Maybe we can just get it to [*insert town we couldn't get it to*]."

With that spirit, we fired up the engine and hobbled forward on our cockeyed, grease-covered tire, hell-bent on making it to Casper without paying for a tow. The plan was to ride the shoulder with our flashers on, going approximately seven miles per hour, pulling over every couple hundred yards to "let the burning rubber cool down." I rode the entirety of the first mile with my upper body out the window, watching that tire spin like a wobbling top as I white-knuckle-gripped the window frame.

By the second mile, we were back outside of the van, sitting cross-legged in the gravel. "We're not gonna make it to Casper, Bri," Neil said quietly.

He spent the next twenty-five minutes on hold with roadside assistance while I stood with my foot in dried cow shit on the side of the freeway, wondering, yet again, what the fuck we were doing with our lives. If you ever meet someone who's lived on the road, and they tell you they have never had this moment, they're lying. There is almost a statistical certainty that if you choose to make your home out of a rolling square of steel and bolts, you will, at some point, watch that home being slowly loaded up onto the back of a flatbed tow truck. You may not be simultaneously standing in cow shit, but I wouldn't rule that out either.

Neil and I were no strangers to breakdowns. Sometimes it was a stroke of bad luck and sometimes it was due to my own recklessness, my undying love for a van that most folks would have taken to the salvage yard years ago.

For example, on a hundred-degree August day, we were barreling down a sixty-mile dirt road having just come from a quiet corner of Lake Powell. We had carried our kayaks on our backs down a steep canyon carved into the rock by early Mormon settlers and paddled out into the inky green water with Bucket between my legs and Dagwood between Neil's.

On the way back toward civilization, we had already spent hours lumbering over high-clearance terrain, so when we finally reached a stretch of smooth road, Neil picked up speed. We must have gotten up to thirty miles per hour or so, because hot air was blasting through the windows of our already air-condition-less van. "Maggie May" was playing on the stereo.

Very suddenly, a deep rut in the road snuck up on us, and there wasn't a chance in hell that Neil was stopping in time. I braced my hands against the dashboard as all four of Bertha's tires left the ground. A desert edition of *The Dukes of Hazzard*.

The jolt was so violent, it sent Bucket and Dagwood flying up from the bed and into the ceiling like two kids in the back of a school bus on a speed bump. I was sure Bertha would crack clear in half. Once I realized the engine was still running, I looked at Neil and shouted, "Fuck! Keep going!" When we turned onto the paved road forty miles later, all four of our driver's side leaf springs cracked off and went skittering across the asphalt.

That was entirely, and unmistakably, our fault. But this just seemed to be an absurd problem to have. Who can't keep the tires on their car? After an hour and a half of silent weeping on the side of the highway, Neil's phone rang, displaying an unknown Wyoming number. It was our tow truck driver. He said he was driving around and around looking for our Honda Element, but he just couldn't find it.

"Honda Element?" Neil asked.

"Yes sir, I got here that I'm lookin' for a blue Honda Element," he said, flatly.

"Um, no, not at all. We're in a huge orange van," Neil said.

"Oh, that thing? I drove past that a couple times, man, that's a sweet rig you got there!" the driver exclaimed excitedly. When met with total and utter silence, he quickly responded that he would circle back and be right there.

The driver—a portly man with a friendly smile—arrived shortly thereafter and spent the next few minutes walking in circles around the van, bent over with two-thirds of his butt crack in the breeze. After first incorrectly attaching one of his tow hooks to our transmission mount, he eventually got it sorted and dragged Bertha's steaming corpse up onto his flatbed.

Due to the shortage of space inside his truck's cab, Bucket and Dagwood awoke from their nap to find themselves being slowly lifted up into the air inside the van. Bucket maintained eye contact with me from the passenger seat the entire time, as if waiting for an explanation as to why she was being abducted.

Once inside the truck, our downright jovial driver began regaling us with stories of how well he does in this particular part of Wyoming.

"'Lotta breakdowns in these parts," he murmured over the clicking of his blinker. "Some folks think it's 'cause of the witches."

He had my attention now.

"The witches?" I asked.

"Oh yeah," he said, "Lots of 'em live up in those mountains there, legend has it. The kids like to go up there lookin' for 'em."

Neil responded with an overly enthusiastic, "Wow!"

That was Neil. Never one to make someone feel out of place or out of line. When I told him any old story, he leaned in as if I were reading Kerouac. It is one of the things I loved most about who he used to be. He made people feel extraordinary.

After a short trip through a dismal part of town, we pulled up to a tin shack in the middle of a junkyard with a small sign that read AAA ROADSIDE COMPLIANT PARTNER. Despite that being a phrase from our insurance website, it also appeared to be the only "name" this shop was operating under.

As the driver lowered Bertha back onto solid ground, men with oil-slicked foreheads and greased-up fingers came out to watch. They whooped at the sight of her, their eyes fixed the way a construction crew's are when a beautiful woman bounces by.

That was the funny thing about Bertha. Even when she was driving us mad, we still had to smile and nod when strangers gathered around to tell us how incredible she was. The owner of the shop signed some papers from the tow truck company and motioned for us to get anything we might need out of the van before he put it up on jacks. I slid the side door open and the first two things we needed leapt out on their own. I balanced my laptop and a blanket and some beer from the cooler in my arms while Neil pulled the camp stove and propane can out from the back. We were starving and we suspected we would be there for a while.

Leaning up against a wire fence, we sat side by side boiling water for mac and cheese while Bucket and Dagwood roamed about, pleased to be in the last of the day's sunshine.

Those dogs were always having a blast, as only dogs can do. The way they saw it, that junkyard was just as good a destination as any. I have spent countless days wishing I could muster just one-third of the enthusiasm they had for absolutely everything.

At dusk, we made our way inside the shop. The waiting room more closely resembled a dorm room with its posters, well-worn faux leather couches, and out-of-date television. Bucket leapt up onto the couch and made a few crunchy-sounding circles before plopping down in a pile of fur. I glanced up to see if the woman behind the counter noticed, or better yet, even cared at all.

With Dagwood on the floor by my feet, I pulled up the email from the South Dakota Tourism team to review the trip schedule. Approximately forty-five minutes from that very moment, we were set to photograph the sunset in Badlands National Park, which would have been lovely had we not still been four hours away from Badlands National Park. I typed out an overly detailed email about what luck had befallen us. My instinct was to assume people didn't believe me. After all, I'd spent nearly a year prior "working" from my van, which was really just me sending one email in the morning and disappearing into the desert for the remainder of the day. I apologized to the tourism team with the intensity of someone whose karma had caught up with them.

It was nearing 9:00 p.m. now, and the crew out in the garage banged on every bolt in Bertha's front axle while I lay curled up on the waiting room couch crying to Neil. "This is a fucking disaster! No one is going to offer me a job again," I said, as if this were the most important thing in the world, as if the South Dakota Tourism Department were the end-all, be-all of opportunities. I was—and still am—brilliant at taking things from zero to catastrophe.

There was no way we were going to get to South Dakota that night, but tomorrow was still plausible. The owner of the shop said he would have no problem repairing and replacing the entire wheel bearing; he just couldn't tell us why it had near-exploded in the first place. Ignoring Neil's hesitation, I said in a panic, "Just fix the bearing, we'll figure the whole thing out later."

Neil dropped his head to his hands, visibly frustrated.

Moments later, the owner's wife popped in to say she was ordering a pizza for the guys. "Let me get you two somethin'?" It sounded like she was telling more than asking. Thirty minutes later, she bumped the door open again with her hip and dropped a cheese pizza on the table with a wink before carrying the rest out to the garage.

Mechanics always seemed to be so kind to us. Perhaps they got a kick out of our whole scene, or perhaps they figured they had to be, since having Bertha in their shop technically made them our landlord too. Whatever the reason, there is a winding trail of auto repair shops across the Mountain West whose teams I still know by first name and coffee order.

This particular shop owner had been kind enough to offer up their couches to us overnight if they couldn't finish, but not two hours later, he walked in smiling ear to ear. "All set," he smirked, tossing Neil the keys.

By then, the entire garage crew knew where we were headed and why we were headed there. None of them had ever heard of someone having a job on Instagram, but nevertheless, as we loaded the dogs up into Bertha, they shouted out suggestions for pit stops and backwoods attractions to make up for the ones we had lost. Neil backed the van out slowly as I blew kisses to all of them out the window.

It was 10:45 p.m. We may have missed sunset, but sunrise was still an option. Neil took the first shift.

Four hours later, he shook me awake, whispering that he couldn't keep his eyes open a moment longer. It was nearly 2:30 in the morning. I got up and drove until 5:00 a.m., glancing in the rearview mirror at my sleep-deprived family in a pile behind me . . . at how strange the passenger seat looked when it was totally empty. Even when Neil wasn't there, one of the dogs usually occupied that spot.

To allow for as much quiet as possible, I played music through my headphones, pressing shuffle again and again until the perfect song came on. Neil Young's "Unknown Legend" seemed like middle-of-the-night music, so I set it to repeat and stared out over the wheel. *The chrome and steel she rides, colliding with the very air she breathes.*

The choice I had made bore consequences that reached well beyond me. I was the one pursuing this bizarre career, this self-sustaining life between internet and open road. Neil had his own career and his own properly working vehicle. In these scenarios, he was just a pawn on the side of the freeway with an angry wife on the run from something.

Sometimes I think we weigh down the people we love most when we're trying to learn to carry ourselves. The scars from that remain like scars of childbirth; evidence that something beautiful was made, but not without taking its toll. I had begun to take a toll on Neil. That empty passenger seat was haunting. The only thing that pulled me from my thoughts was the sudden sound of rain on the windshield.

By the time I pulled Bertha up to the entrance of Badlands National Park, the sun had already risen, though that hardly mattered since it was hidden behind torrents of rain. I threw on a windbreaker and stood outside of the van, trying to take a video of the welcome sign. My finger was so cold, the phone wouldn't even register its touch.

By the time Neil was zipped up and standing beside me, I was practically crying laughing. The kind of laughing when laughing is the only thing left to be done.

"Come visit South Dakota if the Wyoming witches don't get you first!" I shouted sarcastically over the thundering of rain on Bertha's hood.

I considered emailing the tourism department again to let them know it was raining before realizing that they lived here and were likely well aware of the current forecast. The lack of sleep was getting to me.

Back in the van, Neil sat cross-legged on Bertha's floor space, prepping a Jetboil to make hot water for coffee. I opened the schedule again, as if staring at it long enough would somehow undo the fact that we were more than half a day behind.

The heavy rain had subsided to a consistent mist by the time we started Bertha's engine back up and officially crossed into the Badlands. All that water had caused thick clay waterfalls to pour down the creases of the sharply eroded spires. They streamed out onto the black pavement like chocolate milk. The prairies that surrounded the saw-toothed pinnacles of mud were teeming with life in the midst of the storm. Prairie dogs flitted from hole to hole while big-horned sheep ground grass from side to side, staring idly at our passing vehicle. Bison dotted the horizon with their telltale mountainous manes. On this wet and gloomy weekend, we tourists were far outnumbered by the locals.

I leaned out the window, attempting to take any worthwhile photographs or record videos where it wasn't too obvious how freezing and frustrated we were.

On the other side of the park's loop road, we stopped in a tourist-trap town and ate warm donuts and read plaques on the walls about the great bison massacres of the 1800s.

Cowboys on train-tops would open fire on vast herds of them, picking them off with ease. When one bison in a herd is killed, the other bison gather around it, perhaps out of confusion or grief or fear. Either way, it made the act of mass murder incredibly simple. White men hunted them near to extinction by the end of the nineteenth century. Old, grainy photographs show piles of bleached bones as high as a house. They wanted the pelts for rugs and the bones for glue and the skulls for decorative flair. Leave it to modern man to go out and decimate the natural world so they can display its remnants in their living room.

That night, we stayed in a little Snow White–like cabin on the edge of the Black Hills, but Neil spent the whole evening outside beneath

Bertha's front axle, looking for the answer to the problem I didn't give the first mechanics enough time to find.

After rolling slowly into the tiny town of Spearfish, we were back on the side of the road with another smoking tire. A group of local college students who followed me on Instagram careened their car to a halt at the sight of Bertha dwarfing their tiny streets.

They offered to drive Neil to an auto parts store so he could attempt to replace the wheel bearing himself this time. By the time he got back, another student—an aspiring photographer—asked if he could take some photographs of us while we sat there immobile, surrounded by tools.

I tried to play it cool, but I knew Neil was beyond uncomfortable. He never enjoyed being in front of the camera. Even the most effusive extrovert would struggle with having their low points documented in real time, but that was the path I had chosen for me, and in doing so, I chose it for him as well. If only I'd seen this so clearly at the time.

The following two weeks were a nonstop montage of misfortune. I had hobbled us through the South Dakota schedule as best I could, but once that was over, we still had to get Bertha back to Utah.

We had more axle issues immediately upon leaving the bounds of the Black Hills, evidenced by the deep blue crack like a vein in the dashboard from the pounding of my angry fist. We must have blown out some part every fifty miles until we reached Denver, where we spent ten days sleeping on a friend's couch while various mechanics tried to find us replacement parts.

I detailed our situation on Instagram beneath a photo of Neil sprawled out in the dirt beside Bertha's broken body on a barren stretch of plains. The comments had one recurring theme. *Why don't you guys get something newer? Time for a trade-in! Geez, at what point do you call it quits on the old clunker? Is one van really worth this much hassle?*

I didn't show any of those comments to Neil. He'd gotten off the phone with his boss earlier that morning after having to explain why he was missing three weeks of work. It was a phone call he had taken out in the street, and I watched as he paced back and forth on the sidewalk for nearly half an hour.

I knew he would have given up on Bertha right then and there. Most anyone with their head screwed on straight would have. I was far more attached to her than he was. Bertha had become so much more than a van or a house. She was the statement I was trying to make; the embodiment of the risks I had taken. She was proof that I was different, somehow, and I needed desperately to be different. To quit on her felt akin to quitting on myself. After all, I too had been compared to an old vehicle once. Broken down. "Check engine" light blaring.

Neil liked to say that I had become an actual piece of the van, tethered to her with my own rusted joints and intricate wiring just like any other working part. I desperately needed to believe that everything about her was fixable. Because if she wasn't, there was a good chance I wasn't either.

In my dreams, it was a black pickup truck. A newer one with an expensive bike rack on the back. Some city slicker who wasn't used to driving these open stretches of wild dirt. Some guy who wasn't paying attention. I can't ever quite see his whole face. He's wearing a baseball cap pulled low over his eyes. They only look up to meet mine at the very last second, when his truck rolls over Dagwood and rips his insides open across the desert dust.

That is the story my brain lulled me to sleep with in order to survive the horror of the truth. When I was awake, there was no escaping it. There was no black pickup truck, no nameless, faceless man. It was Bertha and my husband was behind the wheel and I was screaming in the passenger seat and our beloved dog was bleeding out in a crimson semicircle, seeping into the sand on either side of him like wings.

. . .

We had driven nearly ten hours already that day, snaking west through northern Nevada before crossing into the southern border of Oregon. When a large lakebed came into view on our right, we turned down one of the narrow dirt roads that led out to it. Despite the lake being dry, it was quite like driving on top of a frozen one. No roads or tracks to follow, just compact clay as solid as concrete and as blinding white as ice.

After a few hundred yards, Neil opened his driver's side door to let Bucket and Dagwood out to run alongside the van. They had a whole day's worth of energy pent up, so they took off like two shots out of a cannon. I watched through the side-view mirror over Neil's lap as they wove back and forth and in between each other like dolphins chasing a ship.

Then I watched Bucket lunge toward Dagwood, playfully grabbing a mouthful of his scruff. Dagwood lost his footing and disappeared from view. The whole van bounced as the back-driver's side tire rolled over his body.

"I hit him, Bri," Neil screamed, "I hit him."

In a panic, we jumped from the van and ran to him. He was howling in pain, desperately trying to drag himself across the sand toward his safe place, toward us and the very van that just maimed him.

He pressed up on his front two legs, but from the waist down he was limp and bloodied. When Neil leaned in to scoop up his battered body, Dagwood reared his head back and bit clear through the soft skin between his thumb and pointer finger. He didn't even flinch.

I dialed 911 on my cell phone. The operator methodically recited the phone number to the nearest emergency vet. It hadn't occurred to me that it was Saturday until the vet's answering machine picked up and directed all emergency calls to voicemail. I pleaded into the phone, begging them to call me back, telling them that we were on our way whether they did so or not.

I typed the name of the vet hospital into the GPS on my phone and looked up at Neil, whose face was white and slicked with sweat.

"It's one hundred and forty miles from here."

"Bri," he said calmly, cradling Dagwood's near-lifeless body in his arms, "you have to drive."

The gravel Bertha's tires were kicking up would surely have shattered any passing car's windshield, but there were no passing cars to be seen. For the first time, I longed for them. I longed for signs of life, signs we were getting closer to pavement and buildings and the emergency vet, whose coordinates still had us over an hour and a half away.

I pressed the gas pedal so hard to the floor that my right hip hovered over the seat. Neil laid Dagwood out on the floor of the van as I swerved violently on hairpin dirt-road turns. He moved his hands slowly down Dagwood's spine, utilizing the medical assessment training he'd received for his job.

One leg was most certainly broken, and he yelped in pain when Neil pressed on the base of his spine before the start of his tail. His groin area was torn open, the skin stripped off like an animal being cleaned for its meat. I could smell blood, taste it even. Like metal that had rusted over. It's a wrong kind of smell, like something I shouldn't have been smelling at all. Bucket lay pressed up against the back corner of the van. I can only imagine what it smelled like to her.

Neil moved to the front seat with Dagwood in his lap, the blood saturating his pant legs. He rolled the window clear down to the frame and propped Dagwood's nose up just enough to smell all the smells he loved. Sagebrush and hot summer air and that chalky layer of dust in the back of your throat. "Stay with us, buddy," he chanted over and over again. Dagwood was visibly in pain, but stoic, calm almost. He would close his eyes every now and again and I yelled out each time. *Please don't. Please don't, Dags. Please don't.* I must have chanted it a thousand times by the time we had even reached pavement.

Somewhere along the drive, the veterinarian returned my call, confidently saying she was ready and waiting for us. It had been over two hours since he had gone under the tire by the time Bertha came careening into the small town of Burns, Oregon. Despite knowing how strong Dagwood was, neither Neil nor I could fathom how he was still alive.

I don't know exactly what I was expecting of the hospital, but I know it wasn't what was in front of me. Small and dark green with wood-trimmed windows. One could mistake it for someone's house if not for the metal livestock ramp leading up to the side door.

The vet held the front door open as Neil rushed past her and into the only room that was lit up. The lobby was dark; the front desk, empty. He placed Dagwood down gently onto a metal exam table. Beneath the fluorescent bulbs, I saw the injuries clearly for the first time. With her hands alone, she told us that he had multiple fractures. When she reached up inside the torn skin, it seemed to stretch translucent like the wing of a bat. Dagwood screamed a scream that sounded human, and I screamed at her to stop.

When she carried him away for an X-ray, Neil and I stood side by side staring at the exam table covered in his blood. For reasons I still don't understand, I reached my finger out and swiped it through the bright red pool. I stared at it on the top of my finger, coagulating, dripping down into my nail bed. This was really happening.

I walked out into the hallway and leaned against a water fountain before my ears filled with cotton and the lights started going black. I slid to the floor and pressed my cheek to the cold linoleum until Neil called out for me.

Back in the exam room, the vet said he had spinal injuries, that his leg had multiple fractures, but remarkably, there was no obvious organ damage. Then, very abruptly, she looked up and said, "There is nothing I can do for him here. He needs blood and surgeons and a whole lot of things that I just don't have here. I know it's hard, but I can put him down for you," she said softly, reaching across to squeeze my shoulder.

I winced back from her touch, and we stood silent for a moment, watching Dagwood's chest rise and fall. She had at least given him her very last and very largest vile of morphine. I pressed my face to his forehead and I begged him to forgive us. The vet never asked us how he'd been hit, but I suspect she understood now. When I looked up from Dagwood's face, she was staring right into mine.

"You could try to make it to Bend," she said softly. "It's another hundred-thirty-or-so miles from here, but there is a major vet hospital up there. I could call and tell them you're coming. I could fax them the X-rays I took."

"Do you think he'll make it there?" I wanted her to lie, but I knew she wouldn't.

She ran her hand over the fur of his neck and whispered, "I do not suspect he will make it that far. But I do think you need to be able to say that you tried."

Neil went to gas up the van while the vet pressed gauze pads to

Dagwood's wounds. She inserted an IV and I held the bag of fluids over him as she wrapped him in a heated blanket she took from a horse stall in the back.

We carried him out to the waiting van, where Neil had laid a clean blanket down and turned the little string of lights on in the back. We used a climbing carabiner to clip the IV bag to the curtain wire over the window. A makeshift ambulance.

With Neil in the driver's seat, I lay down on the bed in the back, face-to-face with Dagwood. Two hours and fourteen minutes, the GPS said. One hundred and thirty-one miles on a two-lane road through high desert and haunting darkness. Neil drove silently, only speaking when he turned around to ask if Dagwood was still alive.

If I squinted, I couldn't see the IV hanging behind him. All I could see were his dark-rimmed almond eyes and his mismatched whiskers and the little cracks in his nose like a fingerprint. We could have been anywhere. Lying in the sand in Mexico, parked at our favorite campsite beside a river, asleep in the cool shadow of a sandstone cliff. I had lain beside him and stared into his eyes like that so many times. There in the dim light of the van, I almost had to remind myself that he was dying.

The lights of Bend, Oregon, came up on us slowly. A couple of houses here and there, then finally a stoplight, which we ran immediately. When Neil turned around to shout that we were five minutes away, I could, once again, scarcely believe that Dagwood was alive. It had now been a little over six hours that he'd been lying broken and ripped open and bleeding.

The reception at the second emergency vet was the first time I felt even the smallest sense of hope. Two vet techs burst through the door with a rolling table—a makeshift stretcher—before we'd even put Bertha in park.

They rushed Dagwood into the back immediately, leaving us standing in the waiting room. With each slow sway of the swinging metal door, his golden ears got farther down the hallway, his eyes still fixed on mine. On the last swish, he disappeared around a corner. It occurred to me only then that I hadn't said goodbye.

The surgeon came out twenty-five minutes later and said he was far too unstable to put under anesthesia, but they were doing everything they could.

They let us in the back room with him only when he had a seizure from the blood loss and they were certain it was time.

I don't know if it's possible for the color to drain from a dog's face, but his telltale desert hue looked almost white. The fur around his eyes was wet and matted. He was so medicated that his mouth hung slack-jawed, the tip of his tongue dry and cracked. Neil dabbed at it gently with a wet paper towel while I sobbed into the fur of his chest.

The doctors felt they had assessed the situation fully. "We can keep trying," they said, "but realistically, there's a less than ten percent chance that he survives this."

Back in the lobby, Neil said he had texted my mom and told her what happened. When the phone rang, I could do nothing but sob into it. "I'm so sorry, Brianna," she said over and over and over again. I walked outside toward Bertha. It was almost 2:00 in the morning at that point, and the vets suggested we try to get some sleep. After all, we had already said goodbye to him. Before I climbed in, I noticed a fresh pile of vomit in the grass beside the passenger door. I knew Neil had tried to hide his fear for my sake, sneaking out there to retch up the grief he was holding in.

The following morning, and once again despite all the odds, Dagwood was alive. He was still too unstable to operate on, but they had begun blood transfusions. One of the vet tech's own dogs was lying on a table, donating the very blood they planned to use.

In a brief moment of calm, I sat out in the lobby, opened my Instagram, and posted an old photo of Dagwood with yellow flowers on his head like a crown. I said that he had been hit by *a* car. Not *our* car. I couldn't say that. I couldn't say *we hit him.* All these years later, I can still barely say that.

I knew I wouldn't have survived those first few days, watching Dagwood die, if what had actually happened had been true; if the two people who loved him most in the world had been responsible. So, I made the truth malleable. I took shelter in the vaguery; believing it would protect me, protect Neil, buy us time. Time to wake up, I hoped, and find it was all just a nightmare and I wouldn't have to say anything to anyone at all. But we never woke up.

I don't know why I posted that photo, or why I went on to document the event in its entirety. I know that I felt wildly alone up there. We were in a town we'd never been to, full of people we'd never met. Neil had disappeared into a world of his own, and I went to my world. Instagram felt familiar. It made me feel some strange sense of normalcy during utter chaos. I clung to people's comments about their own dogs surviving insurmountable odds, about how they had adjusted to life with a severely disabled pet. I needed to talk to someone, to be heard, and hundreds of thousands of strangers showed up to watch, read, and listen.

But amid those supportive comments were cruel land mines I would stumble upon without warning. We were well-known for the freedom we had given our dogs to roam. I could count the number of times they'd been on a leash on one hand in the past year. And so, people immediately blamed us for our recklessness before they even knew how much blame we deserved. *You're a terrible dog owner, letting your dogs go off leash all the time like that. Serves you right for being so reckless. How selfish can you be to put him through so much pain just for attention? You're a fucking monster. You don't deserve to have him survive. You'll never learn your lesson.*

In the first twenty-four hours, Neil and I drained every dollar to our names and called our banks, begging them to increase our credit limit. Veterinary hospitals require money up front for their procedures. Of course, they want to save every dog, but the rules of a human hospital don't apply. You pay up front or you lose your pet.

By the second evening, my mother and a friend created a GoFundMe. She set the limit to $10,000, logged into my Instagram, and posted the link. Neil and I were only made aware of it after she called to tell us it had amassed nearly $32,000 in 12 hours. When I opened the donation page on my phone, the description said that Dagwood was *involved in a car accident.* I remember seeing those words so clearly; feeling them light up my body with shame. It wasn't a lie, but it wasn't the truth either. My mom's reasoning was that she was only trying to help, and it wasn't her truth to tell. So, I let it be. And Neil let it be. And in that silence bloomed that half-truth that would hang between us, heavy and dense; a chain around our necks with the lock on our lips.

I stood from the stiff waiting room chair, walked up to the receptionist, and slid my phone across the counter. "We have the money now," I said. "Tell them to do whatever it takes."

I wish I could tell you that this incredible display of human kindness was enough to send me running to that GoFundMe page to immediately rewrite that line about Dagwood. I wish I had been brave enough. I wish I had known then what I know now: that people would have saved him regardless. But I didn't. I was frantic and shocked and numb and ashamed and disassociated. I watched that money pile up and up and up and I didn't once think of the people who were giving it. I saw only Dagwood in that number. I envisioned him on an operating table with tubes in every orifice, surrounded by surgeons and vet techs and scalpels glossed over with blood. Then a voice on an intercom, mid-procedure, announcing that the truth had come out . . . that all those people wanted all that money back. Every dime of it. The doctors would solemnly remove their masks and leave the room. The lights would dim and the *beep beep beep* of the machines keeping Dagwood alive would grow slower and slower. Then they'd stop entirely.

I wondered if they would at least stitch him closed so we could take him home to the desert to bury him.

I updated my Instagram constantly. With every obstacle Dagwood overcame, more and more people descended on the story.

The people who followed us online started the hashtag #TalkToDagwood. Well-wishers all over the world posted their messages to him, to us. A radio DJ in Arizona shared the story, and had forty-thousand people staring over their steering wheels in the morning on the way to work, talking to Dagwood. News publications began writing stories about this one dog's incredible fight to stay alive. People mailed hundreds and hundreds of cards and packages and gifts to the veterinary hospital. The address was easy enough to find online. For every shift, the veterinarians had a different food delivery, gifted by some stranger. Taco Bell and pizza and boxes of cupcakes and chocolate-covered strawberries that spelled out "Thank You." Someone even dropped off an entire case of top-shelf whiskey one afternoon. Local folks drove by daily, leaving flowers tucked in Bertha's unmistakable door frame, gift certificates for nearby restaurants on the windshield, six-packs of beer on the tire. People emailed us drawings and paintings they had made of our family. Someone called a nearby motel and paid to put us up in a room for as long as we needed to stay. Outdoor brands I had worked with on Instagram in the past made posts on their company pages, wrote articles about the community that was rallying around this "internet-famous dog."

The staff was positively bewildered. It was as though a circus had descended on their little hospital.

When Dagwood stood up and walked for the first time, it was like the Super Bowl. Our trauma was front-page news. And I had put it there.

Whenever possible, Neil and I would go back to our motel room and lie on the scratchy quilt, surrounded by a shrine of cards, and gifts, and dog toys, and paintings, and food baskets. And we'd drink ourselves drunk.

My relationship with Instagram went from light to dark in an instant. I had always navigated this strange online world with a bright-eyed innocence, a fearless transparency. But after the accident, that intimacy felt . . . messy. I felt indebted to the attention, but suddenly enraged by it. These strangers knew my dog, and my van, and my face, but they didn't know what *really* happened. They didn't *really* know me. After Dagwood's accident . . . I didn't know me either. For the first time, the darts people threw in the comments section landed, penetrated my body. And I accepted them because they validated how I had started to feel about myself. It was a small price to pay for Dagwood's life to be insulted by a stranger. In fact, for the first time, I noticed that the insults felt . . . welcome. They felt like penance.

Hurt me. I deserve this. Thank you.

Stella was the first person I told. She had been Dagwood's assigned vet tech the first night he came in, and she hadn't left his side since. She came in on her off shifts, brought her own dog with her to donate blood. When the weekend rolled around, she arranged to move Dagwood to the back room that was normally used for physical therapy. "There're big glass windows," she said. "He can feel the sun."

Dagwood's stomach was still torn open clear down to the muscle in several places. His skin had been hanging open for so long that much of it had died from lack of blood flow and had to be cut off. They were trying to slowly stitch him back up, but were struggling to find enough skin to do so. His tail had been amputated, leaving his rear end looking as swollen as a baboon and bruised the deepest purple I'd ever seen. He had a spiral fracture in his right hind leg that hadn't been operated on yet. Even after five days, he was still too unstable. There, on the soft, padded mat in the physical therapy room, he looked like a prop from a horror movie.

Stella took his vitals or checked some beeping machine what felt like every two minutes. She would adjust his catheter and wipe the feces that were oozing down his backside. The prognosis was that he would be completely incontinent for the rest of his life.

Bucket sat in the far corner of the room. Dagwood was so pumped full of medication and fluids and tubes, she didn't even recognize him. She approached hesitantly, trying to sniff his nose before snapping back and fleeing. He must have smelled so unfamiliar.

Neil had gone to take a nap at the motel, so Stella and I sat in the sunlight together, hovered over Dagwood. She watched me wince each time she adjusted an IV or applied a topical gel. She watched me watching his chest rise and fall, fixating on the numbers on each monitor. I think Stella knew, but I told her the truth anyway. I curled up on the floor between Dagwood and the blue leg of her scrubs, and I sobbed. *It was us. We did this. We did this to him. Look at him. Look at what we did to him.* She patted my back softly and told me it wasn't our fault. It was an accident. Phrases I didn't accept then. Phrases I still can't fully accept to this day.

Stella became our lifeline. She would insist we go nap when we could. She would text us updates constantly, even when she wasn't at the hospital. She went and got drinks with us and told us where to go for breakfast sandwiches, if and when our appetites ever returned.

One afternoon, after Dagwood's leg had finally been operated on and bound together with a metal plate, we got permission for a small field trip. Neil pulled Bertha around to the back of the hospital. I laid clean blankets on a dog bed on the floor space and watched as Stella hip-bumped the door open and carried Dagwood out to the van. Neil supported her back as she stepped up and gingerly laid him down. She smiled and said, "Be back in five minutes."

We drove in circles around the parking lot, going three miles per hour with the windows down. We played "Susie Q" by Creedence Clearwater on the stereo, and Dagwood lay with his eyes closed, the breeze lightly tickling the fur inside his ears. We wanted him to remember what he was fighting to get back to. The home he loved so much.

After a week, we tried to turn the GoFundMe off in an effort to contain our growing guilt *and* the growing dollar amount. But just a few minutes after we successfully disabled new donations, the hospital was flooded with calls from people wanting to donate over the phone instead. Within the hour, the receptionists insisted we turn the GoFundMe back on. Local folks couldn't get through about their *own* dogs because of how many calls the hospital was fielding about Dagwood.

Beyond the sheer inconvenience for the staff, Stella insisted we leave it on for our own sake as well. "At least until he is fully discharged," she said. "I don't think you understand how extensive this recovery is going to be." So that's what Neil and I did—we kept it on and we kept our heads down. Day after day. Diagnosis after diagnosis. Dollar after dollar. If we could just keep Dagwood alive and get our family back to the desert, then we could begin to fully process what happened. Then we might know what to do, what to say, where to start to make it right...

Beyond the horrible guilt that we had done this to our own dog, I felt a horrible guilt over people giving so much to this *one* dog. It was not lost on me that people's human children rarely receive that much help. On Instagram, there were plenty of comments sprinkled throughout the support about how absurd this all was. How Dagwood was *just a dog.* But no dog is ever just a dog.

I understood why people wanted to watch it all, wanted to be a part of it. I wanted to be a part of it too. I wanted to focus only on this outpouring of love from hundreds of thousands of people to one dog and not the fact that our mistakes were the reason he needed that love in the first place.

To raise money to save Dagwood felt almost like an environmental project. Where volunteers and well-wishers would gather around to slide a cage door open, and this once-wounded animal would step back out into the wild.

If we were lucky, he might reach the ridgeline and look back at us just one more time.

In total, strangers from all over the world donated almost $100,000 to Dagwood over the course of three weeks. After surviving a methicillin-resistant staphylococcus aureus infection, five surgeries, two blood transfusions, and twenty-four days in intensive care,

Dagwood was discharged. He had been the longest and most expensive patient in their thirty-five-year history as a veterinary clinic.

His initial diagnosis was that he would be three-legged, possibly paralyzed, and fully incontinent. On discharge day, he walked out on four legs, fully continent, and beaming to be back out in the sunlight. The only thing he'd lost was his tail.

As we drove out of the bounds of Bend, Oregon, and back into the nothingness that haunted us on our way there, I was suddenly overcome with a strange sense of relief. I was glad that the accident had happened so far out in the middle of nowhere. It was terrifying, of course, but if we had hit him only twenty minutes from help, I might have been more convinced that he wouldn't survive. If a veterinarian looked at me, grimly, over the table, convinced the only thing to do was to put him down . . . I might have agreed. But his almond eyes stared right into mine for six hours. Six hours. We had no right to end that fight for him.

When we passed through Burns a few hours later, we called the little rural veterinary hospital to see if the on-call vet was there. When we pulled into the parking lot, it was hard for me to breathe. It had been almost a full month since we'd carried Dagwood in there, screaming and bleeding.

Neil slid Bertha's door open in the parking lot, and the vet climbed in, looking as though she was seeing a ghost. She could not wrap her mind around the fact that he was alive . . . that he slowly stood up to lick her outstretched hand.

For a long time, it was hard to look at Bertha. She'd been the safest place I could think of, and now all I could see were those thirty-three-inch tires. I inspected the driver's side rear tire one afternoon, half-expecting to find chunks of fur or blood, but any evidence of that had tumbled off thousands of miles ago. An eight-thousand-pound van versus a fifty-one-pound dog.

I would wake up to dreams that his head had gone under the tire instead of his hind quarters. I would picture his chest going under, his ribs shattering like an old wire birdcage.

Roadkill was traumatizing. Every mangled deer carcass drying on the side of a bleached highway was Dagwood. The sight of a crushed coyote, its mouth parted slightly and rimmed with blood, sent me into a full-blown panic attack. I had to pull over. I had to remind myself that whoever hit it didn't mean to. It was an accident. I had to convince myself that it did not lie there for hours, dying slowly in the dark.

It was November by the time we made it home to Utah with Dagwood. He still had open wounds that needed stitching and months of physical therapy. Living in a van was no longer an option. For the first two weeks, we slept on the floor in a friend's basement. Dagwood's medication and bandage change schedule had one of us up every few hours, so sleep was scarce.

Neil was able to return to work, but my days were spent with my eyes fixed on Dagwood's chest. Rising and falling. Rising and falling. *Long pause.* Rising and falling. It felt as if someone had handed us a newborn baby and expected that we'd know what to do with it. I was still convinced every breath would be his last.

By December, we moved into another friend's basement and spent three days a week watching Dagwood walk on an underwater treadmill. On Wednesdays, he saw a chiropractor. For as much as I adored my dogs, I never once thought any of them would have a chiropractor. But we intended to spend every penny we received on Dagwood and Dagwood alone.

And yet, as he got better, we got worse. I came home one day to find that Neil had never gotten out of bed. With all of us finally back in Utah, our dog recovering, and his living arrangement situated, Neil was finally free to let go entirely. He no longer had to be the strong one. It became clear that Dagwood's leg was not all that had broken.

I believe Neil was overtaken by the guilt of being behind the wheel, compounded by the guilt of having accepted that kind of money. But I'll never know. He didn't talk about it then, and he's never talked to me about it, directly, since.

Dagwood recovered fully from the accident, though I affectionately referred to his new gait as being "three-and-three-quarter-legged." I don't know that Neil or I ever did. I don't know that Neil or I ever will.

I became so intimately familiar with guilt that it began to eat me from the inside out; force me into a corner where I languished and lashed out like an animal. In the wake of such a public tragedy, we became extreme versions of ourselves. Neil retreated entirely into himself and his own closed-off world.

I, on the other hand, retreated into the world I had created on my phone screen. It was a place of overwhelming positivity, real or imagined. A place where it was much easier to pretend things were okay . . . to pretend we were moving forward, putting this trauma behind us. Dagwood survived, so people saw my life now as a happy story. I spent most of my time trying to see it that way too. It was much easier than seeing the real story that was unfolding in front of me. Neil's beer cans in the shower. His vomit beside the bed. The holes punched through bedroom walls. The flipped over, mangled corpse of the first white pickup truck. Then the second.

Neil was swallowing his feelings and I was sacrificing mine. We had saved Dagwood's life, but at what cost? Neil and I never blamed each other. At least not outwardly. But eventually he stopped coming to bed. I'd find him locked inside a room in the basement with his guitar and his crushed cans. When I'd knock, he would crack the door open, look directly into my eyes, and lie. But each time, I kept my head down and I went back to bed. I kept my head down and I posted. I was certain if I could make our world on Instagram look fine, our real life would follow. *If Dagwood survived it*, I told myself, *then we can too.*

It took me years to say any of this out loud, years to come forward online and admit the truth to everyone who donated. We had all saved Dagwood. But something broke in Neil and I that couldn't be saved anymore.

Sometimes I wonder if we would still be together if Dagwood had died . . . if we had never hit him in the first place. If there had never been a GoFundMe. If there had never been an Instagram for me to fall into. Perhaps the guilt and the shame and the tiptoeing around the truth wouldn't have been so compounded by the prying eyes of hundreds of thousands of strangers.

Many times, I wanted to delete the app entirely, but it felt like people had bought shares in our lives. These people saved my dog's life. I felt I owed them my own in some ways. It felt like people had paid to see a show, and I just happened to have been a tried-and-true performer since I was a little girl. And at that moment, I was dying to perform anything other than the truth.

Two years after the accident, I met Neil at a copy center on Highway 191 in the small town of Moab, Utah. I moved there after we had separated. We signed our names on simple, uncontested divorce papers I had printed off of a government website. In total, it cost us $309 to end our marriage.

Outside in the parking lot, I cried into his neck, breathing in the smell of his old T-shirt. As I wiped tears from my cheeks with the backs of my hands, he handed me a folded yellow piece of paper from a notepad. I recognized it as the one on which he wrote down the songs he used to sing to me.

It simply read, *May the wind fill your sails.* The closing line of a love story ten years long. A whole decade earlier, it was as though he had appeared before me from the depths of my memory. It was comforting to imagine that I could still think of him there. Salt and wind on a summer day. The boy on the sailboat.

When two people part ways, there is an expected splitting of assets. The house and the grandmother's china and the 401(k)s and the holidays with kids. Neil knew the dogs would be better off with me. Or perhaps that I'd be better off with them. But most of the things we had amassed in our shared life couldn't be split in half. Who would get the desert? Who would get the canyons or the campsites? Who would get the rivers and the sunburns and the songs that used to echo off sandstone walls? How could we divide those?

I drew imaginary borders in my mind to make myself feel safe. Moab was mine. The Swell was his. The Roost was mine. Zion was his. There were places in the desert I could no longer go, not because I was afraid he would be there, but because I knew he would not.

Too many things would always feel like *ours*. I could barely drive within a few blocks of the apartment we used to share in Salt Lake

City. And yet, for some reason, Bertha still felt like mine. She had always felt like mine.

I could squint my eyes toward familiar sandstone overlooks and see Neil standing out there in his tattered T-shirt, smiling back at me. But I could hardly remember what he looked like in the passenger seat. I suppose Bertha had belonged only to me for a long time by then.

Neil wanted nothing to do with her in the wake of the divorce.

On our wedding day, Neil and I exchanged small turquoise bands made by a metalsmith who lived in his barn in northern Utah. Together, they cost us four hundred bucks. I'd never been much of a jewelry person, and Neil was constantly removing his anyway for all the rope work he did each week. One evening, after a shift, he met me out at the van in the campsite we'd been calling home for the past week or so. His face was ghost white, tears in his eyes. "I lost my ring," he said. "I thought I clipped it onto my harness with a carabiner but I looked for it everywhere, but it started to get dark and I couldn't find it and . . ." I wrapped my arms around him, breathing in his salt-slicked skin. "It's fine, Neil. It was just a ring."

Perhaps what Neil and I had was something meant to be left out in the wildest parts of the desert like the sun-bleached bones of a once-living thing. I like to imagine that his wedding band is still out there somewhere, buried beneath sagebrush, carried off and coated over with red dirt from the rains; a tiny sliver of turquoise still catching the sunlight every now and again. Perhaps that's where it belonged anyway.

In the early spring of 2020, a young couple driving through southern Utah saw a black and white dog darting across the interstate, narrowly avoiding passing tractor trailers. They made a U-turn over the median and drove back slowly, scanning each side of the dry desert road. They spotted her half a mile back, or so, and pulled off to the side. She bounded toward them from the bushes, her loose puppy skin wriggling side to side, and they scratched her and kissed her nose.

She had no tag but looked decently cared for. She couldn't have been much older than a year. They scanned the horizon and saw a singular farmhouse. After they drove over, the owner opened the door and looked down at the dog with noticeable recognition.

"Is this your dog?" they asked.

Seemingly frustrated, she said back, gruffly, "We don't want her. Why don't you take her?"

The young couple protested, stating their apartment lease wouldn't allow dogs, but the owner had already picked up the little pup and half-tossed her right back into their car.

Several days later, a friend reached out and asked if I would like to come pick up a dog that had been abandoned down south and was in need of a foster home. My life was in chaos at the time. Neil and I were each spending hours and hours a week in various forms of therapy. Neil was so depressed that he could barely bring himself to hold my hand. I felt that I had already lost my husband. It's possible to lose someone not in the sense of death, but in the sense that when you look at them, you can no longer find them at all.

I had no business fostering a dog, but I needed to feel needed by someone. I needed to feel like there was someone I *could* save. I hung up the phone, walked into our bedroom, and asked Neil if he wanted to go for a long drive with me.

It was the last thing we ever did together.

I named her Birdie three weeks later, on the day I decided to keep her. She had a long, hound-like snout with soft little elf ears and one perfect round spot over her left eye. On her back was one big black patch like a horse's saddle. The rest of her fur looked like chocolate chip ice cream.

She was a nervous little thing, though who could blame her. In the first month of her new life, she watched me sob myself to sleep night after night. Then she watched as I threw some stuff into boxes and drove us off to a new house in a town she'd never been to.

Bucket and Dagwood stuck even closer to me after I left Neil, but Birdie barely knew who any of us were. Friends would offer to come take her to the river to swim or to their house to play with their own dogs. I was usually in bed, or a bottle and a half of wine deep; Bucket between my legs, Dagwood curled up against my back. Sometimes I wonder how long it took Birdie to even understand that *I* was her mom.

And yet, despite the grim circumstances under which we found each other, she became the perfect excuse for me to get up every day. Bucket was almost ten; Dagwood, almost nine. They were perfectly content to lie with me for hours on end. But Birdie was just a puppy. She needed to run. It felt cruel to not try to give her the same life that Bucket and Dagwood had always had.

So, most mornings—my eyes still near swollen shut from crying—I would strap my sandals on and head out with all three dogs toward the muddy Colorado River or the sandy cliff edges that overlooked it.

Over time, her timidity turned to unbridled enthusiasm. She would—often without warning—bounce off into the bushes like a deer. She could not enter any body of water without leaping five feet into the air for a dog edition of the cannonball first. Her legs seemed spring-loaded. Her top lip was always getting stuck on her teeth. She was our own little court jester that someone found on the freeway.

Birdie was the first thing that was *only* mine. Neil and I bought Bertha together. We raised both Bucket and Dagwood together from the very beginning. But Birdie only knew Neil for a few days. Regardless, I'll always be grateful he took the drive with me that day. I don't know that I'd have done it if I had to do it alone. Who knows where Birdie would have ended up? Sometimes I like to think that the last thing we did together was just as beautiful as the first.

Step the tires down slowly over the big rocks and remember to keep pressure on the shifter to stay in 4-low. Don't forget to manually lock the hubs or the 4WD won't engage at all. Always tie knots in the end of your ropes, no matter how short the rappel. Start slot canyons early. Afternoons always bring storms. Sprinkle sand on your pots and pans to soak up grease before you wash. Never anchor off a cottonwood tree; their trunks can be surprisingly hollow. Heaviest things go in the bottom of your backpack. In a pinch, you can use eggs to patch a radiator leak, but only the whites, never the yolks.

These are some of the things my husband taught me. I recited as many as I could remember that night I spent sleeping in Bertha in the middle of the road, surrounded by herds of cattle. I wondered what Neil would say if he knew that after all that, I was still out here in the road, alone, in the depths of summer, in that godforsaken broken fucking van.

It was hardly the first time I'd found myself wondering what Neil would think of my predicament. After our divorce was finalized, with snow still on the ground, I packed the van and the three dogs and headed for New Mexico. I was itching to find some warmth. On my GPS app, I zoomed in on what looked like an extensive network of sand dunes far, far from the borders of White Sands national park. I set the coordinates.

The road on the way in was so full of potholes, it was nothing more than a braid of dirt and pavement. I pulled over to pee twice, the spring sun beating down through a bluebird sky, the dry yellow grass tickling the back of my legs. After passing a few dune buggies on the road, I knew I had to be close.

The sand dunes were only slightly taller than Bertha and positively identical in every direction. Dirt tracks wove between them aimlessly, and camping seemed to be designated to whichever spot hadn't been blown away that week. I set up the stove and lit one of the prerolled joints I'd purchased in Colorado on the way down.

The dogs and I wandered in no particular direction as the sun melted down over a distant, dried brown mountain range. The sky was practically glowing in neon purple-pinks by the time I followed our footprints back to the van and climbed into bed.

Around 2:00 a.m., Bucket woke me up, whining and pacing in front of the door. I sat up and took a long swig from my water bottle.

I might as well go pee too. Outside the stars shone softly behind layers of hazy clouds. I stared up at them, resting my elbow on my knee to prop up my chin. I wondered if it might rain the next day.

I climbed back into the van, shooing Birdie off my pillow that she enjoyed stealing as soon as I looked away. Dagwood was fast asleep in the back with his nose propped on a pillow toward the slightly cracked window.

After a few minutes, I called out for Bucket. "Lesssgo, baby girl!" I shouted, in between puffs of the rest of the joint from earlier. Sleep was hard for me to come by after the divorce. I didn't realize how attached I was to *my* side of the bed until I didn't need to have one anymore. But the weed helped.

"Bucket, let's *GO*!" I shouted, more firmly this time.

After another five minutes passed, my heart started to thump a bit harder. Probably from the weed, I told myself. Bucket was just a few months shy of ten years old. She had never run off once. She was nearly sixty-five pounds, smart as a whip, and damn near as fast as her one-year-old sister.

I walked in circles around the van. "Bucket, come *on*, Mama."

She's chasing something, I thought. *It's the only reason she's ever this late*, I told myself. I went down the list. Jackrabbits were more of a sunset-hour chase. Lizards were most certainly not out right now. Maybe some nocturnal rodent dove down a hole in front of her and she was halfway to hound heaven.

I opened the driver's side door and beeped the horn twice. Back in our redneck running days, a beep of the horn stopped Bucket and Dagwood in their tracks. They knew it meant it was time to turn back and load up.

After another five minutes, my temper flared. *Are you FUCKING kidding me . . . This FUCKING dog . . .* Then the weed-induced paranoia crept in. *What if she's going deaf because she's getting older now and she's going to die soon and leave me. Everything I love leaves me.*

Ten minutes later, as I sat silently between my calls to her, an eruption of coyotes yipping and barking and howling burst out from somewhere between the dunes. Somewhere close. I leapt forward from the van door so fast, I faceplanted into the sand. Still on my hands and knees, I shrieked her name in a desperate high pitch. I could feel the skin in my throat crack.

I slid the van door shut and took off running in the direction it had come from. I was barefoot, without a headlamp, and without a phone. I ran, screaming, weaving erratically through the dunes, up and over them, slicing my feet open on the spiky shrubs and cactus that sprouted from the tops.

"*Heyyyyy! Hey! Hey! Heyy!*" I screamed, trying to make my voice as deep, but as loud as possible. I stopped in my tracks, waiting for any sound, waiting for any hint on which way to turn. I spun in the sand, my feet frozen and stinging from how cold it gets at night. A classic case of desert extremes.

Another burst of yips and howls, closer this time. I took off sprinting, screaming her name, screaming expletives. Then I resorted to pleading the way I had pleaded to Dagwood. "Please, no. Please no!! Please no, Bucket!"

It was silent for a long time. Whatever the coyotes had killed was dead. I imagined them slinking back through the dunes with blood matting the fur of their snouts.

I was on my knees. My eyes had adjusted only slightly. The moon was just a sliver and the clouds still made the starlight murky. But I saw her eyes as clear as day. Bucket appeared a few feet in front of me, frozen, as if startled by the sight of me too. When it registered what and who I was, her whole body practically wound up before shooting toward me as if out of a cannon. I sobbed into her fur as she wiggled around between my crouched knees. She was completely unscathed and downright jovial.

I stood up and smoothed my hair back with my hands. "You stupid idiot, Bucket." She stared up at me, smiling, panting. The gray on her snout looked even grayer in the dim light. I bent down to hug her one more time.

As I stood once again, it very suddenly occurred to me that I had absolutely no idea where the van was. I climbed up the nearest dune and scanned the horizon, but it all looked identical. No orange paint in sight. Bertha was a needle somewhere in a one-hundred-sixty-square-mile haystack. I had brought no phone, no headlamp, no shoes, and no jacket. *Why didn't I at least turn the goddamn headlights on.* The goose bumps on my skin felt like cactus needles.

I attempted to follow my footsteps back, but I had been running so frantically, they barely looked like footprints at all. Bucket had been weaving in and out looking for me too, and her footsteps must have crisscrossed mine in multiple directions. The tears started flowing again.

After wandering around unsuccessfully for another hour, I sat on top of a dune. *We only have to survive until morning,* I told myself. *It's cold, but it's not that cold. We probably won't get frostbite.* Just then, the sliver of moon came out from behind a cloud. A few hundred yards away, the light caught Bertha's roof box just right.

The coyotes continued yipping all night. I'd reach out and pat around the bed, half-asleep still, checking for each dog. I'd never *ever* been afraid of that sound before. In fact, it had always been one of my favorites. In my logical brain, I knew my dogs had never gone anywhere near coyotes. I knew they knew not to. I knew the coyotes were out there peacefully moving through the desert in the way they always had . . . in the way we used to. But I had forgotten who I was. I defined myself by my failures; by the vicious words strangers used to describe me. *You're not smart enough to do this. You're not brave enough to do this. What would Neil say. Who else will you hurt with the consequences of your decisions.*

I stared out the window of the tow truck at the passing fields, brown and dried from a whole summer's worth of sun. The driver had arrived approximately twenty-six hours after I had broken down. It was a two-hour drive back to Moab. Normally I would have felt pressed to make conversation, but the driver didn't say a word, so I didn't either.

Near-disasters had always been a part of choosing to live in a van. That wasn't going to change simply because I didn't have Neil to complain to anymore. And, oddly enough, those had always been my favorite stories to tell.

Bertha was the reason I learned how to be alone in the first place. I had become an expert at planning my own trips and packing my own gear and attaching my own propane. I had learned to *love* being by myself out there beneath the red walls and the shadows of the bright green cottonwoods. I loved being someone other women looked up to. I had become so utterly convinced of my own bravery. I had learned to feel proud of myself for continually facing the fear of being a woman, alone, out in the wild.

I laugh now . . . thinking that I knew what it was to be alone.

I wanted to believe I didn't need to give this all up, move back to Salt Lake City, start saving up for a condo. I wanted to believe I could run back out into all those wild places and feel the same sense of safety I always had. I wanted to believe that if I carried on living that life as if it hadn't all fallen apart, then maybe I could convince myself that it hadn't all fallen apart. Maybe I could convince myself that it wasn't all for nothing.

I had chosen to go out and do daring things. So many days, I'd been temporarily wooed by the safety of being just another face in the crowd. Just another cattle in line. There were so many nights I was positively sick to death of having to be my own inspiration.

In those early days on my own in the van, I used to lie in bed and beg for someone to appear to me like a fairy godmother. Someone who had walked an identical path to mine. Someone older and wiser who could assure me they had made all the same mistakes, and then some. I wanted someone to tell me that the path I was walking didn't end in rubble.

Instead, I was simply left with my forehead pressed against the window of a tow truck and all the doubts and the fears and the shame and the anger and the what-ifs and the how-comes. I spent a good long while drinking my fill of that cup. But with every passing mile, I tried to take a kinder look at it all. I had arrived here, wounded and scarred and beaten to hell, but I had arrived here nonetheless. The only thing left to do was to find out why.

The pictures on the realty website could have been any old patch of land. It looked as though someone intimately familiar with documenting kitchen spaces and walk-ins had gotten lost in the desert with a digital camera. Overexposed photos of sandstone. Some slightly sideways shots of juniper trees. A few flowering cacti.

Something about the haphazardness of the listing itself made me less nervous to inquire about it. It didn't come across as too sure of itself, which I liked, because I wasn't too sure of myself either. I had never gone to an open house before, or looked up the nuances of a lot loan. I had never even spoken to a Realtor prior to the day I found myself following one up to that undeveloped nine-acre piece of land on a mesa in southern Utah.

The dirt road was a sharp left off the freeway, but it ran alongside the pavement for at least another quarter mile before cutting up suddenly into switchbacks that traversed the layers of red earth crust.

On the right side of the road, spindly roots of juniper trees stuck out of the wall sideways into the air, as if reaching out for the earth that had been ripped away. To the east, jagged hills, interrupted only by bright red sandstone upthrusts, snaked toward the base of a sweeping mountain range. They were still ever so slightly snow-capped. With one more panoramic sweep, the road crested the top, turning west across a mesa of high desert.

The Realtor, in her clean white sneakers, sidestepped over a pile of dirt rooted down with yucca flowers. There was no floor plan, no new appliances, no talk of the local school district. Outside of having me follow her to the designated boundary line, there wasn't much else for her to do. She leaned up against her car and motioned me onward, like a knowing mother to a nervous child.

I wandered farther away, farther through the junipers. There was a substantial wash that swooped around the front of the property that would act quite like a moat if the desert ever saw that much water. The juniper trees—which I always thought looked more akin to gigantic bushes—were 250 to 300 years old at least. Prickly pear cactus beds grew around the base of them, pillaging all the water they could catch to keep their cotton-candy-colored flowers in bloom. Little blue scrub jays flitted from tree to tree as if chatting nervously among each other. The late-spring sun was still warm enough to make the beetles ring out and the sand buzz with heat.

The back side of the property was an alcove of sandstone rocks with intricate faces and cracks and caverns. I stood with my back against the warmth of them and looked out south beyond the dirt road that led us there. Miles of dry desert hills and coral pink petrified sand dunes and mesas, and the soft blurred edges of the Abajo Mountains.

A driveway would need to be carved out and a well would need to be drilled. A septic tank would need to be buried, and a full solar-powered system installed. I didn't know a single thing about any of that. The doubts started mounting slowly, but reliably, the way the ocean gathers up the beginning of a wave.

But something in my gut told me I could survive this obstacle too. This would be my land, my dream, my idea in the first place. I would be taking this on as a woman *truly* alone. Out here in a place where it seemed even the earth didn't act as one might expect a woman to. *Soft* and *motherly* and *nurturing* are not often the words used to describe the desert. With her dusted walls and barren stretches, she is a prickly, standoffish side of Mother Nature not easily understood. Everything that grows there does so by sheer will. But land that is harsh on the surface can still be easily scarred. An offhanded step into the cryptobiotic topsoil, a slight stumble off a beaten path; these transgressions are not easily forgotten. One footprint in the wrong place can be visible for years, decades even, but with time, things still grow up and around it. Living plants springing up and weaving directly through the bones of the old ones.

I would be tasked with being the caretaker of one delicate little corner of the world I'd spent the last six years in. I was completely overcome with that churning mix of excitement and fear. The same feeling I'd felt in the belly of that boat back east. The same feeling I'd felt when I climbed behind the wheel of Bertha.

I would once again be draining my bank account dry on a whim, because for some reason, that's just who I am. But, this time, I would be giving myself the real roots of the thing I'd lost, the thing I'd subconsciously sought all along in my own stubborn way. At the end of the day, no matter what it looks like, we all just want to go home.

I knew I was going to buy the land the moment I rounded the corner to it. I sat up on those rocks as proud as if I'd clawed my way on bloodied knees right up to the base of them. Dagwood was weaving his way through the rocks and the deep red barrel cactus flowers that had begun to bloom. His scars still visible through his fur. Bucket followed him closely, nose to the ground, while Birdie leapt from rock to rock. Bertha was parked out in the road with some steaming part that would probably fall off in the next week.

Many of the things I loved so deeply were abandoned or broken in some way, and that made me love them more. Isn't that what I'd preached all along, after all? Things did not need to be shiny or new or perfect to be worth having, worth saving. The most old and rusted and broken thing I'd ever had was the thing that got me home. Like a tin man on a yellow brick road.

We'd all arrived here like most living things arrive in the desert. Wrapped in all that beautiful red sand, bleached by the sun, swept through the painted canyons, and displaced by the rushing of an unexpected flood. But with time, wherever they end up, those surly roots slip back into the ground as if they'd been there all along.

Weeks later, when I signed the title to the land, the loan officer gave me a large folder containing my copies of the paperwork. On its cover, a nicely laminated photo of a white picket fence. An irony that wasn't lost on me.

When my father heard about the land, he called to congratulate me. In the wake of my divorce, we began speaking more frequently. He'd been sober for two years by then. Sometimes I'd call and we'd chat, awkwardly at first. The power tools and background noise of his jobsites could always be counted on to cover uncomfortable silence. I pictured him in faded blue jeans, leaned up against his black truck with his phone to his ear, a thin layer of sawdust covering it all.

I would send him photos of the dogs on my paddleboard, or Bertha on a 4WD road in the desert, or a sunset I was slightly unnerved to be watching alone. He had barely even heard of social media. I wasn't a figure on Instagram, dead set on proving all the beautiful, worthy parts of my life. I wasn't "the girl who hit her dog." I wasn't one half of a love story with a tragic end. I was no one to him besides his daughter.

He would write back, "How'd you get to be so cool?!" or "Wish I was there with you! We would be listening to the Dead!" I smiled, imagining how long it took for him to type those texts, squinting down over his nose at the screen.

"Nine acres, Brianna, wow," he said, laughing nervously into the phone that afternoon. "You know, I'm a carpenter, in case you forgot . . ." We ended the call with the promise that he would fly out to Utah someday to help me build my house.

By then, I'd lived in Utah for nine years. He had never flown out before. But perhaps now, he saw where he could fit into my life; where he might feel useful to a now-grown child. I could be more like a client and less like an estranged daughter. I could accept his offerings on a contractual basis, skirting around the lifelong stubbornness that kept me from him in the first place.

I imagined our hands, spindly and long-fingered—his nine and a half and my ten—on our knees in the dirt digging out the foundation. Perhaps my mom would be off in the junipers somewhere, pulling up dead shrubs and roots with her floral gardening gloves. Perhaps they would tolerate each other's company for only the second time in my adult life; the first having been my wedding day.

I didn't feel my father deserved to walk me down the aisle, but I couldn't bring myself to tell him that. I've always had a penchant for protecting the feelings of people who've scarcely protected mine.

I walked barefoot through the grass toward Neil in that champagne-pink dress, my father's calloused hand looped through my right arm, my mother's delicate fingers laced around my other. We had all begun to cry at the top of the hill, so my mom leaned over and whispered, "Quick, John, you have to make us laugh." He proceeded to recall the story of the hairless rat I tried to sneak home in my backpack from that old seedy pet store, and we giggled with tears still in the corners of our eyes. Then we fell silent as we started walking, overcome with the gravity of the moment.

Perhaps I should have been thinking about Neil standing there with his long hair and bare feet on top of the living room rug we decided to use as our altar. But all I could think was that I wanted to walk slower. I wanted to dig my heels into the ground and beg, like I had so many times as a child. *Just one more story. Just one more story.*

But I let them go. I hugged and kissed them both, and I let them go.

That was the last time I have ever been alone with my mom and dad.

Even if my dad *did* come out to help with my house, my thirty-year-old mind knew it would be nothing like what the child in me still imagined. There would be heavy machinery and crews and blueprints and architects. But when it came to him, I was a child frozen in time.

I pictured him hunched over, shirtless, gingerly sliding plywood over a table saw in the driveway of the little blue house; my eyes fixed on him, waiting for instructions. My mother watching us from the lace-curtained windows. *Flathead screwdriver. Hammer. Wrench.* My little hands would go digging furiously through the toolbox. I could only identify a few of them, yet those always just happened to be the ones he needed.

In my mind, that's how it would go. My father and I somewhere between the juniper trees and the desert sky with nothing but a pile of tools and all the years' worth of things we'd never said.

It was well over one hundred degrees. The dogs and I were headed toward the river, where I'd plop a camp chair down directly into the murky, lukewarm water. I had stopped to lock Bertha's hubs before the road devolved into deep sand. The engine was running loud and hot, echoing off the narrowing canyon walls. But I still heard it. The unmistakable pounding of hooves.

For a moment, I thought the dogs had jumped through the open windows and taken off after a mule deer, but they sat staring straight ahead in the front seat. When I turned to scan the field behind me, I saw it. A few hundred feet from the van, amid heat rising up like steam from the sand, stood a white horse.

We stared at each other silently. The dogs had not yet noticed. Quite suddenly, the horse took off running straight toward Bertha, straight toward me. I pressed my back to her hot orange paint as it got closer, kicking up dust with a confident trot.

Years earlier, Neil had nearly been trampled by wild horses, resorting to climbing a lone cottonwood tree to escape their beating hooves. By the time the white horse reached the van, I had positioned myself on the other side of it just in case. With each step it took toward me, I took one backward. I kept my eyes fixed on it out of caution and the bizarre belief that if I blinked, it might disappear. It might have never been there at all.

We wandered in slow, hesitant circles around the van, peeking out around the corners at each other as if playing a game. There was no brand on its flesh, no marks from a saddle. Healed scars stretched across the skin between its eyes. Maybe it was wild, but maybe it wasn't.

In small desert towns, it isn't uncommon for animals to disappear from pastures overnight. People would drive out to the edge of a high desert field, open the doors to their trucks or their trailers, and dump their sick horses and their old dogs right there.

Some folks just can't afford them anymore, but they don't want the neighbors to know that they can't afford them. Better for them to simply up and disappear one day. We're always so worried about the neighbors.

But this horse didn't look sick. It didn't look injured or old or starving. The muscles rippled across its chest, as if dancing beneath the skin. Its eyes shone so black, they looked blue. It had found its way to the only water source around for miles, the only green grasses until the border of Colorado.

Though logic told me otherwise, I wanted to believe that horse ended up there of its own volition. I pictured it bursting through an old, rusted gate that had held it in place for most of its life, sprinting down the streets of the one-light towns toward the open desert plains.

I think about that horse sometimes. About the starkness of its glowing white hide against the red of the sandstone. It looked out of place, and yet somehow, it didn't at all. Like a girl from Connecticut, sitting cross-legged, alone, atop a cliff in Utah on nine acres of wild land that now belonged to her.

The smaller I set out to make my life, the bigger it became. I struggle with that sometimes . . . with the conundrum of it all. The life I lived was simple, but it was also extraordinary. Peaceful, but also chaotic. It was messy and painful and beautiful. Even the parts that were over now.

One night, soon after I bought the place, I woke up to the glow of the moon outside and climbed out into the night. Bertha's orange paint looked yellow in the starlight. The dogs were fast asleep and the sand was still warm from a full day of desert sun. I wandered barefoot through the sagebrush and fallen juniper branches, dried and twisted as if frozen by wind. I tilted my chin upward, my hair swaying against my naked back. Constellations were so bright, they almost appeared closer than the moon. The Milky Way tore through the sky directly overhead, a halo of other universes and stars bursting out from either side.

There were no streetlights, car horns, no sounds at all. Just the vastness of a night sky that had never once been drowned out by humankind. I lay down beneath it all, crossed my hands over my chest, and closed my eyes. And I smiled, remembering a long-ago little girl peering out of a moving car at the glow of someone's tiny windows in the foothills of nowhere.

Who the hell would want to live all the way out here . . .

ACKNOWLEDGMENTS

I am forever indebted to the hundreds of thousands of strangers who saved my dog. To Dagwood's surgeons: Dr. Dahlberg, Dr. Parchman, Dr. Dougherty, Dr, Bottorf. His Emergency Room team: Dr. Lacey, Dr. Stone, Dr. Kitagaki, Dr. Scavuzzo, Dr. Abraham, Dr. Bunting, and every other team member at the Bend Veterinary Emergency Center. And to Stephanie, for the love you poured into Dags day after day.

Every pawprint Dagwood has left in red sand since that day, I owe to all of you.

To my mother, for all the things you were, and all the things you weren't. I am who I am because of both of those beautifully complicated things. To my father, for trying in the times I felt I could not. And for still calling me Goose. And to my brother, for being the co-keeper of my secrets. I am so proud of the father you are today.

To William, for the penny, the clover, and the ring.

To my agent, Abby Saul, for spending the last four years in my corner as the story you signed on for changed into the story you made me feel brave enough to write. And for your Monday morning check-ins, signed each time with: *I'm here, as always.*

And to my editor, Sydney Rogers, for knowing the truths I needed to tell and carrying this ever-evolving story with unmatched tenderness and understanding.

My respect for these two extraordinary women is immense.

I am so grateful to my entire team at HarperOne: Sarah Schloof, Aly Mostel, Makenna Holford. Your enthusiasm for this book made all the difference.

To the amazing friends I've had all my life. You know who you are. Thank you for letting me burn down the things that needed burning, and waiting for me there when I climbed back out from the ash.

To Mr. and Mrs. D for believing in me always and for being the home I could run to when my own collapsed.

To Ms. Pastorak and Professor Portman-Daley. This book exists because many years ago, you told a kid she could be a writer.

Lastly, as of the publication of this book, I must acknowledge that the care with which I crafted parts of this story . . . the truths I chose to tell and not tell . . . the agonizing honesty I valued so much in the completion of this book . . . These things were all deeply intended for a person who I now know will never read it. There is an altered version of this story that better suits their need to survive it. And that's okay. The truths here in these pages exist now for me only. As they should have all along.

Regardless, I will remember you always as that boy on the sailboat.

ABOUT THE AUTHOR

BRIANNA MADIA has been telling stories all her life. Her first foray into writing was a neighborhood newsletter at the age of six, eventually leading to a BA in writing and rhetoric many years later from the University of Rhode Island.

Since then, Brianna has been living a life of relentless intention in the deserts of the American Southwest. She made a name for herself on social media with inspiring captions-cum-essays about bravery, identity, nature, and subverting expectations. She currently lives on a plot of land in Utah with her four dogs. *Nowhere for Very Long* is her first book.